Live organic

Live organic

Brilliant ideas to purify your lifestyle and feel good about it

Lynn Huggins-Cooper

Careful now

Organics, and the organic way of life, have become mainstream, no longer associated with knitting your own yoghurt and mud (of course, if you do knit your own yoghurt from mud, this book has something to offer you too). We've all become much more aware of the environment and of our impact on it. Here you'll find suggestions for reducing your impact on the world, and reducing the impact the modern world has on you. Keep an open mind, be careful, be informed and tread lightly.

Now, though the contents of this book were checked at the time of going to press, the Internet is being updated constantly. This means the publisher and author cannot guarantee the contents of any of the websites mentioned.

Copyright © Infinite Ideas Limited, 2008
The right of Lynn Huggins-Cooper to be identified as the author of this book has been asserted in accordance with the Copyright, Designs and Patents Act 1988.

First published in 2008 by
Infinite Ideas Limited
36 St Giles
Oxford, OX1 3LD
United Kingdom
www.infideas.com

A CIP catalogue record for this book is available from the British Library

ISBN 978–1–905940–57–8

Brand and product names are trademarks or registered trademarks of their respective owners.

Designed and typeset by Baseline Arts Ltd, Oxford
Cover designed by Cylinder
Printed in India

The paper and board used is chlorine free and was produced from sustainable forests. This book was printed using vegetable-based inks.

Brilliant ideas

Brilliant features

Each chapter of this book is designed to provide you with an inspirational idea that you can read quickly and put into practice straight away.

Throughout you'll find three features that will help you get right to the heart of the idea:

■ *Here's an idea for you* Take it on board and give it a go – right here, right now. Get an idea of how well you're doing so far.

■ *Defining idea* Words of wisdom from masters and mistresses of the art, plus some interesting hangers-on.

■ *How did it go?* If at first you do succeed, try to hide your amazement. If, on the other hand, you don't, then this is where you'll find a Q and A that highlights common problems and how to get over them.

Introduction

Wherever you look, the news is overflowing with terrifying stories about the carcinogenic effects of additives in food, pesticides in our fruit and veg, cumulative poisons in our drinking water and foul fumes from our furniture. It can make you feel that everything is hopeless and you are surrounded by dangers. Now, the problems are there, but you can take control. Take action and you can start to filter the chemicals and toxins from your life – and the lives of your children – step by step.

I first started thinking seriously about the poisons that surround us in our cosy homes and gardens when I had my first child twenty-one years ago. Having a precious new life to care for brings everything into sharp focus. When I insisted on breastfeeding, and making all my own chemical-free baby food, I was out of step with the norm. Today, organic baby food is available on the high street and there are cookbooks and kitchen appliances designed to help you. 'Organic' has gone mainstream; it's no longer a word associated with a hippie, knit-your-own-lentils lifestyle. You can now buy organically produced clothing, furnishings, furniture, make-up, bath supplies, cleaning supplies – and that's before you even get started on the food!

Consumer demand for organic food has grown rapidly over the last decade. Organic food sales in the UK, for example, have risen to over two billion pounds a year according to the Soil Association. At present, demand is outstripping supply, and farmers are converting to organic farming techniques in large numbers. Everywhere, people are digging vegetable beds and growing their own food. You can't get fewer food miles than that!

People are looking for organic alternatives for environmental and health reasons. Overwhelmingly, consumers have rejected GM foods and are choosing organic – preferably local – foods for fresher, better-tasting meals. Animal welfare is high on the agenda, with free-range egg sales rising dramatically. In the UK during 2008, for instance, the sales of free range and organically produced eggs outstripped those of eggs from caged birds for the first time. This proves that consumer power drives change – and that, as consumers, we vote with our feet.

As you'll see, organic products have moved beyond the niche market. Organic box schemes are springing up everywhere, with food taking a direct route from the field to the plate. Public support for locally produced, seasonal organic food is ever growing. People are thinking about food miles, and buying near to home boosts the local economy and reduces your carbon footprint. Consumers are becoming aware that shopping is an environmentally charged act. There are many people providing organic alternatives to conventional products now, and I mention some of them in this book. You'll find contact details, including web addresses, for these suppliers in the Directory at the end. If you find something you like online, but the supplier can't send it to you or you'd prefer not to have things shipped some distance, then use the websites to inspire you to find a more local alternative.

There is one area which needs more consideration, and that is the issue of organic meat. The question here is not 'should I eat organic meat?' but 'should I eat meat at all?', and this is why you won't find any chapters about organic meat in this book. Evidence of the environmental impact of eating meat is overwhelming. A Japanese study from the National Institute of Livestock and Grassland Science in Tsukuba looked at beef production. They found that producing a kilo of beef results in more CO_2 emissions than going for a three-hour drive while leaving all the lights on at home, producing greenhouse gases with a warming potential equivalent to 36.4 kg of CO_2. Most of the gas emissions are a result of methane from belching cattle.

That's in addition to the chemicals often used to force pasture – 340 g of SO_2 and 59 g of phosphates are used to produce each kilo of beef; most meat production is not organic – and these chemicals can have devastating effects as they run off into river and lake ecosystems. The more demand there is for meat, the more deforestation is needed to create new pasture, and the livestock sector takes up 30% of ice-free land on the planet already. A 2006 UN report called raising animals for food 'one of the top two or three significant contributors to the most serious environmental problems, at every scale from local to global'. It suggested that it should be a major policy focus when dealing with problems of land degradation, climate change and air pollution, water shortage and water pollution.

Apart from pollution, we need to think about ethics. Setting aside the arguments about whether it is ethical to slaughter animals for meat, there is also the question of world hunger. According to the British group Vegfam, a four-hectare farm can support sixty people growing soy beans, twenty-four growing wheat, ten growing corn and only two farming cattle. In *Diet for a Small Planet*, Frances Moore Lappé tells the reader to imagine sitting down to a 225 g steak, and then imagine the room filled with forty-five to fifty people with empty bowls in front of them. The feed cost of the steak is the equivalent to giving each person a bowl of cooked cereal grains. Do think about it.

You may want to go organic, but it may also seem overwhelming. Don't try to do everything at once. Baby steps, added together, can take you a long way. It is easy to start making a difference; I've done it, and so can you. Start with the small things that fit into your daily routine, and remember that doing something is always better than doing nothing because you feel overwhelmed. Before you know where you are, you'll find yourself living a healthier, simpler, cleaner life. Our own small steps, taken as individuals, join us together with others all over the globe – marching towards an organic and sustainable future.

1. Let us spray?

Organic: it's a term that's emblazoned on packaging (minimal, of course) and shrieks from chic menus – but what does the term 'organic' really mean? Learn to decipher the jargon.

'Organic' seems to have become synonymous with 'quality' in the eyes of the purchasing public – take a walk through any supermarket and look for the proliferation of labels. But why?

Organic food tastes better. There's a sweeping statement for you! I grow and buy organic food because I know that I am not putting a wide variety of potentially harmful chemicals into my body, or into the bodies of my family. But I also enjoy it because it has a distinctive taste.

Organic food is also grown and produced with care, and a good way of buying it is to join a box scheme. Food which is bought in these 'brown box' schemes, where the food is mainly sourced and grown locally before being delivered to households on a regular basis, tends to be very fresh and seasonal. This helps to remind the people who join the schemes of the passing of the year and the rhythms of the seasons. Now, the fruit and vegetables in the box may sometimes come with blemishes or munch marks from bugs and slugs – and won't have the

1

Here's an idea for you...

Find out more about organic producers near you, and if there are any brown box schemes available locally. Don't be afraid to shop around as some are more expensive than others and quality can vary.

uniformity of regular shop-bought produce; the shapes can be hilarious and sometimes obscene – but they will have a fuller flavour because they are produced as nature intended. This kind of food isn't forced into tasteless growth out of season; it isn't artificially inflated by growth hormones or chemical fertilisers. In addition, it may be cheaper to buy organic food from a box scheme than from a supermarket – and they usually have the added bonus of cutting down food miles, as your food is less likely to have to travel far from its producers.

For food to be certified as organic, it has to be produced according to strict guidelines. In the UK, the Soil Association is the main body concerned with the certification of organic produce. When you see the Soil Association mark, it means that the product so marked has been produced without herbicides (weedkiller) and only a limited range of pest-control measures such as derris (an extract made from the roots of several tropical and subtropical plants), soft soap (which contains fatty acid potassium salt, made from bone and palm oil) or the naturally occurring materials sulphur and copper. The remedies which are allowed by the Soil Association have been found to disperse safely and do not persist in the food chain, unlike many conventional chemicals. They are also used rarely, as organic producers prefer to use biological controls such as nematodes, ladybirds and lacewings to control pests. Organic growers also use barrier methods, such as covering crops with fleece or other materials.

Organic food producers pay attention to enriching their soil and fortifying it naturally. They do not use artificial fertilisers; instead they use green manures (basically growing nutrient-rich plants which are ploughed back into the soil), organic animal manure and plant-based concoctions, such as liquid comfrey or seaweed extract, to feed the soil. Genetically modified crops or ingredients are not permitted in the production of certified organic products, and animal welfare is also an important part of certification.

Of course, non-foodstuff organic products are also available. They include clothing, household goods and personal care products. As we become more aware of the possible dangers of chemical saturation in our lives, more and more of us are turning to organic produce to create a balanced lifestyle.

Along with chemical weapons, chemicals used in farming are the only substances that are deliberately released into the environment designed to kill living things. They pose unique hazards to human health and the environment.

Soil Association

How did it go?

Q. When I look round the supermarket, the organic fruit and vegetables are much more expensive than standard goods. Why is this?

A. Organic production is labour intensive. I know that with back-breaking certainty, as I hand weed acres of garden! That means it is more expensive for growers, who need many more human hours to produce a crop than conventional producers do, with their large-scale herbicide and pesticide crop sprayers. As organic farming tends not to be intensive, yields tend to be lower. We are also spoiled by cheap food produced by conventional farmers receiving subsidies from the government. As government responds to the increasing public demand for organic produce, more subsidies will likely become available to support sustainable organic production methods – and that can only make organic goods cheaper for consumers. Do remember that there are also hidden costs – as far as the cost at the checkout is concerned – associated with conventional methods using artificial fertilisers, such as cleaning up pollution when 'run off' enters water courses. In the UK, it has been estimated that this costs around £120m a year. We pay for it via taxes and higher water bills.

Q. If organic farmers are allowed to use pesticides, then how does that make them any different from other growers?

A. The pesticides used by growers certified as organic are minimal, disperse quickly and have a low impact on the environment. Many of the pesticides used by conventional growers are the opposite – they persist in the environment and may have very harmful effects on animal and human health. Conventional, non-organically certified growers in the UK are permitted to use around 350 different pesticides. The UK's Soil Association estimates that around 4.5 billion litres of them are used annually.

2. Mindful eating

What's in your food? Before you push another forkful into your mouth, can you say for sure that there are no nasties lurking in the lettuce or hiding in the hummus?

Here's how to identify your enemies.

It seems that with every day's news we hear about more things in our environment that are bad for us – in the air we breathe, the water we drink and most of all in the food we eat.

News reports of alar in apples, GM crops, food irradiation, BSE in beef and dioxins in milk are enough to put you off eating for good. But is it really that bad? Intensive farming methods have been used extensively to maximise production in recent years. This is not because farmers are intrinsically a greedy, profit-focused bunch; it is because it has become increasingly difficult to make a living as a farmer and many businesses – often generations old – have, sadly, failed.

Intensive production relies on the use of herbicides (weedkiller) and pesticides to boost the production of crops. Intensive farming methods are used to increase milk and egg yield, and to promote faster growth of meat animals. Such methods mean that livestock often lives in cramped, stressful conditions. Apart from animal welfare considerations such as the de-beaking of hens to prevent pecking and the docking of tails and trimming of teeth in piglets, cramped conditions make disease more likely to take hold and spread – and this leads to the routine use of antibiotics and other drugs.

Here's an idea for you...

Find out about the chemicals present in your everyday life, and also those which are in many brand-name pesticides, so you know exactly what you are dealing with. Then you can start a campaign against them from an informed position. Remember that consumer power is a driving force for change and write to the companies that provide the goods you buy. Then write to your local politicians, to newspapers and magazines, and spread the word.

Such factors, together with chemicals used to increase shelf life in food, means that we as consumers can end up taking in a cocktail of potentially dangerous chemicals, albeit in small doses, every time we eat a meal. Combined with the pollutants found in our water and air, these chemicals may build up over time and may well have long-term health implications.

Many pesticides and herbicides such as organochlorides (OCs) and organophosphates (OPs) have been linked with the development of diseases and disorders such as cancer, fertility problems, birth defects, immune system deficiencies, nerve damage and ME. And it's not just the chemicals sprayed on the food you actually eat that you need to worry about. As chemicals are sprayed in a fine mist, they travel in the air. This means that they enter the air we breathe, and settle on unsprayed areas. The chemicals are walked into our houses on our feet, and residues may be found on the carpet the family lounges on to watch TV. The chemicals are also leached off into the soil by rain, enter watercourses – and thus also enter our drinking water.

The chemicals that enter our bodies can stay there in our body fat. The organochloride DDT has been banned for many years (in the US since 1972; in the UK since 1986), but traces are still found in human breast milk, animal milk and in the body fat of Arctic penguins.

And it's not just the dose of pesticide that needs to be considered when we assess danger. The timing of the exposure is crucial. Doses of pesticide seen as safe in a healthy adult will have a different – harsher – effect on more vulnerable people such as babies in the womb, children, teenagers and the elderly.

This all makes frightening reading. What we need to do is to become better informed. We need to read the news reports (even if they scaremonger) and keep up to date with current research into the effects of chemicals on our bodies. Only once we are well informed can we make the choices that affect the health of ourselves and our families.

What we don't know can indeed hurt us.

Joseph Lieberman, US Senator and campaigner

How did it go?

Q. I have read about chemical residues in breast milk and wonder if this is true or just another scare story. Should I bottle feed my baby instead?

A. In 1999, a WWF report warned that babies in the UK were being exposed to over 350 artificial contaminants via breast milk, and were ingesting up to forty times the World Health Organisation's daily limit of hormone-disrupting chemicals. Despite these figures, the WWF still recommend breastfeeding as the best option. Not only does breast milk contain all the nutrients a baby needs for optimum growth and development; it also boosts the immune system. Of course, babies fed on bottled animal-derived milk are also exposed to pesticide contaminants, as the animals may also have chemical residue in their body fat.

Q. Surely if pesticides are allowed to be sold and used, they must be safe. Isn't this all just another thing that it's become fashionable to worry about?

A. It depends what you mean by 'safe'. In the UK, for example, the Pesticides Safety Directorate (an Executive Agency of the Department for Environment, Food and Rural Affairs) works to ensure the safe use of pesticides for people and the environment and the Independent Pesticides Residues Committee monitors residues in foodstuffs. Theoretically speaking, this should ensure that all pesticides used are safe and used safely. However, even if you accept the view that various pesticides are safe individually (many researchers don't), it's worth considering the degree of safety offered by a cocktail of different chemicals. US researchers found that when they combined three chemicals, proven to be 'safe' when used at the recommended levels and alone, toxicity rose to dangerous levels.

3. Naughty but nice: organic chocolate

Most of us enjoy a square of chocolate now and again. But did you know that non-organic chocolate may contain traces of the pesticides lindane, methyl bromide, naled, glyphosate, hydrogen cyanide and pyrethrins?

Does that bar look as tempting now?

Non-organic cacao (from which chocolate is derived) is mainly produced by plants grown in unnatural conditions, often planted in direct sunlight although cacao naturally prefers shaded conditions, under the rainforest canopy. That means that the plant grows under stress and is more susceptible to disease, making the use of pesticides 'necessary'. Cacao plantations are often fumigated with methyl bromide, a carcinogen. The Pesticide Action Network say that, as a crop, cocoa is second only to cotton in the amount of pesticides used during production.

Now, when the plants are grown in the shade they are less likely to suffer from infestations and therefore the 'need' for pesticides is greatly reduced. Organic chocolate producers such as Green and Black's are organically certified and do not use chemical pesticides or fertilizers. Such suppliers often (but not always – it is worth checking) support Fair Trade and thus benefit the cocoa producers, so that the workers receive a decent wage and their communities benefit from

Here's an idea for you...

If you really fancy a treat, try to source some single origin or single bean organic chocolate. This chocolate is made from one type of bean, from one supplier, even from one particular plantation. Chocolate connoisseurs believe that this is the ultimate chocolate experience. Why not give it a try? Some suppliers, like Montezuma's, make several varieties of delicious single-origin chocolate bars. This type of chocolate isn't cheap – but nor are single vineyard wines. And if it costs more, you'll buy less, and save your waistline!

investment into clean water supplies, schools and other vital resources. Organic chocolate manufacturers also produce their confectionary using cocoa grown without herbicides. But chocolate isn't just cocoa, of course, and organic producers use certified organic sugar, fruit, nuts, herbs and spices as well.

Worldwide, the sales of organic chocolate are booming. The UK's organic chocolate market is the biggest in the EU with sales of around £18m in 2005. In the US, there is also a huge demand with sales there having increased by 49% in 2006 alone! The Global New Product Database from the market researchers Mintel shows that 170 new organic chocolate products were launched across the globe in 2007. And the large companies are now joining the rush, which was led by smaller independent suppliers, to grab a piece of the organic chocolate action and make sure they have a share in this expanding market. In May 2005, Cadbury Schweppes controversially acquired the trailblazing Green and Black's brand, and Hershey bought Dagoba in October 2006.

Perhaps organic and fair trade chocolate, although more expensive than regular confectionary, is a product people are willing to buy as it is already a treat or luxury – and is therefore worth the extra cost. In terms of costs to the environment and even to the health of the gourmand it is even more worthwhile.

Dark organic chocolate – a magic bullet?

Organic cocoa gives chocolate a richer flavour, but there is another reason for eating dark organic chocolate beyond what the industry calls 'mouthfeel': it's good for you! It really is; dark chocolate – with over 70% cocoa solids – contains high levels of antioxidants called bioflavonoids. These help to combat free radicals, which can cause damage to the cells in your body. Antioxidants help your body to reduce toxins and limit the cell damage that can cause premature ageing and diseases such as cancer. Free radicals accumulate with age, so it is important, as you mature, to up your intake of antioxidant foods such as blueberries and green tea – with a little red wine and dark chocolate to follow. Dark chocolate actually contains more antioxidants than either green tea or blueberries – but of course it also contains fats and sugar, so don't get too carried away!

All you need is love. But a little chocolate now and then doesn't hurt.

Charles M. Schultz, US cartoonist and creator of *Peanuts*

How did it go?

Q. I've been hearing a lot lately about raw cacao powder – it's being touted as some new superfood. Is it really all it's cracked up to be?

A. Raw cacao powder is being hailed as one of the most powerful antioxidant foods ever – but just because it's being hyped doesn't mean it isn't great. Raw, unsprayed cacao powder is the untreated version of cocoa powder. Laboratory analysis has found that the raw chocolate powder has 955 ORAC (Oxygen Radical Absorbance Capacity, a measure of antioxidant level) units per gram. That's more than any other food surveyed including famous antioxidants such as green tea. Try adding a spoonful to smoothies, brownie mix or milk to make a delicious food that does you good as well as tastes good!

Q. I'd like to try this but I've had a quick look around and I can't see any organic chocolate in my local shops. Isn't it difficult to get hold of?

A. Not as difficult as you might think; in fact even major supermarkets are beginning to stock it, though usually just the brand leader. Try a supermarket and if you can't see it on their shelves, ask – if you don't, your supermarket may just assume there is no local demand. Health-food shops are also worth trying; they often carry several different brands, and you may well find a wider range than you'd encounter in even the largest supermarket. Failing that, do some searching online. You'll certainly be able to feed your cravings with a clear conscience.

4. Home-made heaven

Organic food is all very well for a treat, but how can you cook organic food on a regular basis without having to take out a bank loan?

Here's how to get the best from organic food without bankrupting yourself.

I have found that since I switched to all organic food, I have been cooking more 'proper meals'. I have come to the conclusion that this is for a variety of reasons. Firstly, it's because you know the food you are using is of such good quality that it deserves to be treated well and prepared in a way that exploits the premium flavour of organic food – and that makes you want to cook a good meal, so you reach for the cookery books. Secondly, if you sign up for an organic box scheme you get a variety of vegetables each week that can tax your inventiveness and make you think about cooking foods you wouldn't necessarily seek out, or hadn't thought about. Then there is also the issue of 'ready meals'. If you embrace the concept that you are going to cook organically for your health and the health of your family, you are less likely to buy ready meals, which are traditionally full of fat and made from highly processed food. There are organic convenience foods such as ready-prepared vegetables, and baked goods such as quiches and pies, but they tend to be expensive.

Here's an idea for you...

Baking freezes beautifully. When you make a quiche, it is very little extra effort to make a second for the freezer – you've already got the ingredients out and made the mess. Make a second fruit loaf when you bake, and slice it before freezing. That way, you always have fresh baking for unexpected guests or just for yourself when you need a comforting snack with your cuppa.

With a little thought and advance preparation, organic cookery does not need to be any more difficult and it can save you a lot of money. I have found that I am actually spending less money on food as I rarely go into supermarkets these days. I grow food, supplement it with a box scheme and buy things such as pasta, pulses, bulgar wheat and couscous in bulk from an ethical wholesaler. Not going into the supermarket means you are not seduced into buying food 'on special offer' or any of those 'three for two' deals that you do not really need. I have noticed a lot less waste in the fridge at the end of the week since I have not been trawling the supermarkets. My family and I have benefited in terms of health and well-being – and also in terms of more varied dishes. I get a real sense of satisfaction out of seeing my family eating food that I know is not only tasty, but is as free from worrying chemicals as possible.

Convenience food

I'm not saying you need to turn into some sweet little lady (or man!) in a pinny, always covered in flour and smelling of baking. But lots of nutritious organic food is really quick to prepare. In our house, pasta is the fast food we grab on a busy day. Think about it – how much effort does it take to chuck pasta in a pan of boiling water, and to make a quick sauce out of plum tomatoes, onions, mushrooms and olives? Our second standby is soup, and I make at least one large vat a week. Red lentil and potato is a favourite and really fast: chop an onion and a few potatoes and boil them in a pan of water flavoured with organic bouillon. Add a bag of red lentils and that's your soup, and I sometimes add other veggies such as carrots or sweet potato. Super-fast food!

If you batch cook and make a double batch of food, you can freeze a portion ready for the night when you can't be bothered – which will come. That's a really good habit to get into, and will help you to avoid grabbing poor-quality ready meals. Pasta sauce, soup, chilli, curry, stew, goulash – anything in sauce such as these meals freezes really well. Freeze the food in a variety of portion sizes so that supper for one is available as well as a full meal for the family. That means it's easier to cater for people coming in at different times and with different commitments. Finally, don't forget to label your freezer containers!

You don't have to cook fancy or complicated masterpieces – just good food from fresh ingredients.

Julia Child, US cooking guru

How did it go?

Q. *Well, I get an organic veg box, and it's great – except I've had parsnips for weeks now, and then there was the time of the turnip. I've run out of ideas completely and everyone's going on strike. I'm tempted to give up. What can I do?*

A. This can happen. Firstly, don't get fed up and cancel your box; get creative instead. It's another chance to break out those cookery books. If you've exhausted your own supply, get down to the library or just search online – try 'parsnip recipes' and you'll end up with about 50,000 possibilities. How about a chickpea and parsnip curry, or parsnip chips with a cucumber and yoghurt dip? (There's even more choice when it comes to turnips, amazingly.) Don't let this get you down; remember food is seasonal and work around it.

Q. *I'd like to go on an organic cookery course to give me a jump start with my cooking. What can you recommend?*

A. There are lots of options, and if you search the Internet you will find something to suit you, both in terms of content, cost and location. A great option, for instance, is Penrhos Court, a gorgeous old Herefordshire manor farm on the Welsh borders where Daphne Lambert, author and cookery expert, runs Greencuisine organic food and cookery courses. Many similar places offer an equally good opportunity to combine a holiday in beautiful surroundings with learning a new skill, so hunt out something convenient.

5. Water palaver!

How can water not be organic? When it's full of pesticides, heavy metals and other baddies, that's how. Find out how to clean up your act.

Our bodies are made up of around 70% water. To maintain our health, we need to drink at least eight glasses of water daily, or one cup for every 9 kg of body weight.

Our water supplies come from surface water such as lakes, reservoirs and rivers, and ground water such as aquifers (underground sources). Pesticides can enter the water supply as they run off land into rivers and streams. If rain falls on treated land before pesticide has been absorbed properly, that pesticide can also enter surface water. Rain and snow has to travel long distances in streams and rivers before it is collected to process as drinking water. Pesticides can also filter down into groundwater and contaminate drinking water supplies, and can drift in the air when applied, contaminating water when they land. Pesticides also enter the water supply when they are dumped illegally, either during industrial use or by householders pouring domestic pesticides down the drain. Antimicrobials – a type of pesticide designed to kill water-borne diseases – are even added to the

Here's an idea for you...

Think seriously about buying a water filter. Jug filters, the ones that you keep in the fridge, are useful and remove some impurities from water. Under-sink or tap filters are the next step up and you can buy basic ones quite reasonably. Reverse osmosis water filters involve forcing water through a very fine membrane under pressure. This removes everything dissolved in the water, so you get very pure water indeed. The 'top of the range' water filters are expensive, but in terms of health may be worth it. Do your research and check out the Internet for prices.

water when it is treated prior to drinking. Pesticides are sometimes even applied to lakes and wetland to kill weeds and insects, and this pesticide then enters the water cycle. Although there are guidelines on the amount of pesticide that is 'safe' in drinking water, it is widely accepted by researchers that there are no safe levels. This is especially important when the effect upon overall health of cocktails of chemicals ingested from a variety of sources such as air, food and via cosmetics is considered.

Pesticides in water can disrupt the nervous and immune systems, cause liver damage, cancer, kidney damage and birth defects. Pesticides do not usually kill immediately, but accumulate in body fat and cause problems over time.

Bottled water isn't necessarily safer than tap water, either. It may in some cases be even more contaminated than tap water as there are less stringent checks. Bottled water is marketed cleverly – and quite cynically – to emphasise its purity, which may not actually be the case. In addition to that, bottled water can hardly be seen as a 'green' option.

It's big business; huge companies such as Coca Cola and Nestlé are now part of the market. Sales of bottled water have exploded over the past two decades. Over 89 billion litres of bottled water are sold in the developed world each year and half of this is sold in Western Europe. Some 20% is sold in North America, and sales in South East Asia are growing. Between 1999 and 2004, there was a worldwide increase in sales of nearly 50%.

The extraction of water for bottling can cause local water shortages and can potentially damage the ecosphere, depriving organisms of the water they need to survive. In addition to this, there are other environmental costs. The bottled water industry uses around 2.7 million tonnes of plastic in packaging each year. Most of this plastic ends up as waste which may be buried in landfill sites or incinerated. The production of the plastic uses fossil fuels, as does the transportation of the water for distribution.

It is worth looking for the 'greener option' packaging-wise if you are buying bottled water. PET (polyethylene terephthalate) is increasingly being used for water bottles instead of PVC which is a good thing as it can be recycled into many different products, such as fibres to make fleece jackets and coats. When incinerated, it does not release chlorine into the air, which many plastics do including PVC. Glass water bottles can also be recycled or reused.

So what else can you do? Well, you could buy a water filter for your house, and if you want to have water on the move buy a reuseable bottle rather than refilling a plastic one. Old plastic bottles aren't designed to be reused; the chemicals in them can eventually leach into the water. When it comes to bottled water, the Soil Association does not certify water as it is so 'mobile' and difficult to monitor. It is suggested that if you want to buy bottled water, you buy water from springs on certified organic land, which is also bottled in its natural state, without treatment. It should come from an officially registered source and conform to purity standards.

More energy is encapsulated in every drop of good spring water than an average-sized power station is presently able to produce.

Viktor Schauberger, writer and ecologist

How did it go?

Q. Is it better to use bottled water than tap water to make up drinks for my toddler?

A. Some mineral waters have a very high mineral content, which makes them unsuitable for young children and babies. Sodium (salt) is particularly dangerous as babies and young children cannot excrete the excess and may sustain kidney damage. It has been suggested that bottled water should be labelled to say this, to avoid health problems. It is safer to use filtered tap water which has been boiled and cooled.

Q. Is it worth using a jug filter, or do they just remove limescale?

A. You tend to get what you pay for. The cheapest filters may just remove hard deposits, but many jug filters do remove heavy metals, bacteria and even pesticides. Read the literature that comes with the jug carefully to find out what is removed by the (usually carbon) filter. You can also buy kettles with integral filters so that every cup of tea or coffee is free from potential contaminants.

Live organic

6. From vine to wine: organic wines and spirits

A chilled glass of Pinot Noir; a rich plummy Merlot or a light, fruity Zinfandel… lovely. But hold on, because there are hidden nasties even in the nectar of the gods.

There are more than just grapes in the average glass of wine.

Azinphos-methyl, myclobutanil, dicloran, dichlofluanid, dimethoate, diazinon, phosalone, chlorpyrifos-methyl, vinclozolin, carbaryl, methiocarb, parathion-ethyl, triadimefon, procymidone, iprodione, imidan, dicofol. It sounds like the chant of a mad scientist, but unfortunately it's a list of some of the pesticides regularly used during wine production. And the things that are added to the grapes then end up in the wine we drink.

In the UK alone, people drank an amazing 1.2 billion litres of wine in 2004 – and that means 25.4 litres per person. That's a lot of wine – and, unfortunately, that means a lot of chemicals. Recent studies have shown that most wines are contaminated with pesticide residue. One study of Bulgarian wine even found that wine from an industrialised region contained more than double the legal limit of the heavy metal lead.

Here's an idea for you...

Host an organic wine tasting – enjoy yourself and spread the organic message at the same time. Get in a range of six or so red and white wines and invite some friends round; you don't even have to tell them the wines are organic (you can remove the labels – keep a list and number the bottles instead – and spring that one on them once they've realised how good they are). You'll probably find the after-effects of this kind of evening much less painful, too.

The problem is that vines are vulnerable to red spider mites and fungal growth and are regularly sprayed as protection and treatment. The way that vines are grown, close together for a high yield, means that pesticide is 'needed' to support these intensive growing conditions. This is the case across France, in the Bordeaux, Burgundy, and Champagne regions; in Australia, in Chile and Portugal. Chilean wine often shows high levels of contamination with pesticide, perhaps due to the inadequate training of the workers who are using them.

A similarly grim picture is painted of vineyards in California, shown in the report *Rising Toxic Tide: Pesticide Use in California*, 1991-95 published by the Pesticide Action Network. It found that pesticide use increased by 31% in the five year period. Over 22 kg of pesticides were used per harvested 4000 square metres. Many pesticides were being used near rivers which were sources of drinking water, the Russian and Napa Rivers, and 90% of the world's domestic wines are produced in California, so this pesticide usage spreads around the globe as the wine is shipped and consumed. In California itself, grape production has been blamed for a third of all pesticide-associated illness in the state. Workers are exposed to pesticide residue on the vines, and there is a high incidence of dermatitis and skin inflammation.

Worryingly, unlike food, there is no legal obligation for wine producers to list all included additives on the label. Common additives include sulphur (a preservative), ascorbic acid, tartaric acid, and isinglass (derived from fish and used to clarify wine). Many of us remember with horror the 1985 fiasco when Austrian wine was found to contain an antifreeze – diethylene glycol – as a sweetener instead of glucose. It was added because it was cheaper than glucose – and you can bet that wasn't declared as an ingredient on the label…

Green glass?
Wine is shipped all round the world from wine-producing areas. That means heavy liquid contained in heavy glass travels great distances. Fossil fuels are used to transport the wine, adding to its carbon footprint. The UK imports twice as much green glass as it manufactures – and most of that is made up of wine bottles. Although lots of glass is recycled, it still accounts for 7% of household waste.

What's your poison?
Have you ever woken up, clutching your forehead after a night of wining and dining? It could be that the chemicals in the wine are to blame, rather than the alcohol. It has even been suggested that the fact that our morning-after headaches increase with age is the fault of pesticides. The idea is that there is a cumulative effect, and that the pesticides stored in your body fat increase over the years, magnifying their effects. It would be worth putting this to the test by trying organic wines, and seeing if there is a difference in the way you feel the morning after.

Organic wine production

In organic vineyards, the soil is fed with compost, manure and organic fertilisers to make it nourishing for the plants that grow there, and biological control is used for pest problems instead of pesticides. The vines are often underplanted with other plants that encourage beneficial insects. The organic wine industry is experiencing a surge in demand and sales are rising by 20% a year. Environmentally conscious consumers are buying more organic products in their weekly shop, and that now includes wine. Organic wine has a very 'real', fruity taste and the aroma has no chemical whiff about it, like that of some conventional wines.

Wine is bottled poetry.

Robert Louis Stevenson

How did it go?

Q. I think I get a reaction to sulphites as I get headaches and flushing after drinking wine. Are organic wines sulphite-free?

A. Winemakers have added sulphites to wine for centuries as this prevents the wine from going off. Most conventional wines have sulphite concentrations of between 50 and 200 parts per million. Sulphites cause problems for around 5% of the population with allergies who experience your symptoms as well as rashes and cramps. Some organic producers add sulphites; others do not – you'd have to ask. No wine is completely sulphite-free, though, as sulphites are naturally produced when fermentation takes place. However, organic wines are generally lower in sulphites, so they may be a better alternative for you.

Q. I'm confused. Are organic wines really a greener option?

A. Well, yes. Apart from the obvious benefits of no pesticide use, organic producers often embrace other environmentally friendly practices. Bonterra wines are a good example. They bottle their wine in recycled glass, print their labels using soy ink, and use tree-free paper. It's worth checking, so you can drink your wine in a cloud of smug righteousness.

7. Conscious cleaning

Feeling the need to blitz-clean your house? Before you reach for the bleach – stop! There are milder organic alternatives.

Conventional cleaners get the job done — they deliver whiter than white baths, limescale-free toilets and windows that gleam. But at what cost?

Cleaning solutions used routinely in the home contain many potentially dangerous chemicals, especially when they are used together. Here are some of the dangers lurking in the cleaning cupboard:

- Alkyphenols – multisurface cleaners; may disrupt hormones
- Chlorinated compounds – bathroom and tile cleaners, pesticides; may cause immune system disruption, and reproductive/endocrine disorders
- Phthalates – air fresheners and multipurpose cleaners; may cause reproductive disorders and birth defects
- Aromatic hydrocarbons such as naphthalene and trichloroethane – deodorisers, air fresheners, all-purpose cleaners; could cause damage to the central nervous system and are possible carcinogens
- Butyl cellosolve – metal polishes, de-greasers; can irritate upper respiratory system and cause liver/kidney damage.

Have you noticed the smell in the cleaning products aisle at the supermarket or in your cleaning supplies cupboard? These chemical-filled products evaporate into the air even when they aren't being used. You know they are harsh when you are using them because of the way they make your hands sting and go red, and the way the fumes make you choke and your eyes water.

You don't need to use artificial chemicals to clean your house. My eldest daughter experienced severe allergic reactions to some, especially floor and multisurface cleaners. Once I realised what was causing the reactions, I looked for greener cleaners. I discovered the many dangerous chemicals found in cleaning supplies and haven't bought them since. I've found that milder organic cleaning fluids take a bit more effort and elbow grease, but they work. I'm also safe in the knowledge that they won't pollute our indoor air or the environment when they are disposed of. Taking small steps in your everyday life is the most effective – and lasting – way to reduce your impact on the environment.

Greener cleaners

If you decide to make the switch to gentler products, it needn't be expensive. Many manufacturers are producing eco-friendly, plant-based cleaners. Some are available from supermarkets and health-food shops, but for a good selection try many of the online collections.

Here's an idea for you...

Learn how to read labels. It sounds simple, but consumers have little to go on beyond warnings on labels. If it has a big cross or toxicity warning, don't use it. Don't be misled by vague words such as 'natural' or 'botanical' or pictures of plants on labels. Many such products haven't even seen a whiff of a plant-based ingredient. Even if they do have a few drops of essential oils they tend to contain chemical nasties unless they expressly state that they don't. Learn to look for buzz words such as:

plant-based
no nitrates
no phosphates
no chlorine
no petroleum products
no solvents.

You can also make your own cleaning supplies. White wine vinegar is great for windows and degreasing surfaces. The smell of the vinegar disperses as soon as it evaporates, so your house isn't going to end up smelling like a chip shop! For a really lovely smell, soak lavender or rosemary in the vinegar – just add a sprig to the bottle and replenish as necessary. I use a cheap plant mister to spray the vinegar for use. It is a great disinfectant too and can even be used as a great fabric softener. Add a quarter of a cup of white herb–infused vinegar to your machine's rinse cycle and you'll have a lovely smell too.

Bicarbonate of soda is another cleaner your great-granny would have been familiar with – we call it green; it was what she was used to using. Make a paste with lemon juice and use it to clean stains from kitchen work surfaces; use it with vinegar – soda first, then the vinegar – to make a plughole cleaner that won't destroy the environment as it strips out accumulated grease deposits. This mixture can be added to hot water and used to clear drains, too. For a mildew remover, dampen a cloth with a vinegar/water mixture. Sprinkle bicarbonate of soda on the cloth and scrub; it gets tiles really clean. Don't forget to keep up air flow in damp areas and that will help to keep mildew at bay.

I hate housework! You make the beds, you do the dishes and six months later you have to start all over again.

Joan Rivers, comedienne

How did it go?

Q. I have dogs, teenagers and a partner with smelly sports shoes – so I've used a lot of air freshener in my time! I've recently been thinking about how bad it is for the environment, and for our health. What can I use as an alternative?

A. Firstly, remove the source of the odour. That doesn't mean putting the family and the dog out with the bins! Make sure animal bedding is washed regularly and that rooms are aired frequently. If you still need to use an air freshener, think about heating organic essential oils which release natural fragrance into the air. A lovely alternative is to simmer cloves or ginger in hot water on the stove. This fragrance is especially lovely on a cold winter day when you might not want to open a window.

Q. I picked up some oven cleaner the other day but after reading about the toxicity – on the product label – I put it down again quickly. What can I use that won't make me retch as I use it?

A. To clean a really crusty oven, make up a bicarbonate of soda and vinegar paste. Spread it over the surfaces and leave overnight. The next day, scrape what you can off the oven with a wooden spatula and wash the oven thoroughly with hot water and a little lemon juice. Once it is clean, line the bottom with foil (make sure you don't touch the element if it is an electric oven) to catch spills.

8. Pond power

Adding water makes any garden more relaxing and beautiful. Forget the pond chemicals you see in garden centres – with an organic pond you can build a healthy ecosystem and ditch them.

A pond is a wonderful addition to any garden.

To read some books and articles, you would think you have to have a chemistry degree to maintain a healthy pond. Many pond keepers use algicides, herbicides and pesticides in vast quantities, creating more problems than they solve. If you look at a healthy, wild pond you will see a balanced ecosystem. This is what you are aiming for in your garden. If the ecosystem is balanced, you do not need chemicals. Adding a pond to your garden will help you in your drive for an organic lifestyle as the wildlife it attracts help to remove slugs, snails, aphids and more from the garden without recourse to chemicals. Birds – and mammals, such as hedgehogs – are attracted to the water for a drink, and then hang around to munch slugs and snails. Dragonflies will take care of the mosquitoes, and frogs and newts will gorge on slugs. All this is, of course, aside from the pleasure you will get from watching your new pond as the seasons pass.

Creating a new pond

When you first dig your pond, think carefully about where it is situated and save yourself many problems; this will help you to avoid the use of chemicals when maintaining it. It's very important, for example, to site your pond to avoid any overhanging vegetation. When leaves fall in the pond, they rot and release minerals and nutrients into the water. That sounds good – but it's how the water ends up looking like pea soup in spring. The rotting leaves can also silt up the pond, making water levels drop. That means fewer differing habitats, so less wildlife. And it's the pond wildlife, such as frogs, dragonflies and newts, that help to kill pests in the garden and help you to avoid those chemicals. A silted-up pond also warms up too much in the summer and freezes too easily in winter.

Once you have found a site (for example, I have a very large pond and an increasing number of satellite ponds near veggie patches to keep slugs down through the natural predators), work out the size of liner you need. There's a handy formula: length plus twice the maximum depth multiplied by width plus twice the maximum depth. Buy the best liner you can afford. Butyl is very durable and lasts for years. When you are digging the hole, make it a few inches deeper than the pond to allow for padding. I have used wet newspapers, carpet and sand. Make sure you leave a shallow beach area covered with shingle for small creatures to get in and out; it also allows the organic gardener's friends – the hedgehog, the blackbird, etc. – to drink easily and safely. As you dig, lay the rich topsoil to one side; you can use it on the garden. Keep some of the poorer subsoil for back filling on top of the pond liner. Lay the liner

Here's an idea for you...

Avoid algal blooms in your pond with a battery of organic weaponry. Some algae is required for a healthy pond but if it takes over, it can choke your pond. Making sure you have enough plant cover is the first line of defence. Then make sure you have algae-eating animals such as pond snails – readily available from garden centres. Once introduced, they breed like wildfire! Add a raft of barley straw. I tend to hurl in a handful, tied with a piece of barley straw as binding, but you can buy neat little squares from garden centres.

on top of the padding, and cover it with a 5 cm layer of subsoil. Bury the edges of the liner and then slowly fill the pond with water.

Don't be tempted to add water-clearing chemicals at this point. At first, the pond will bloom green with algae but hold your nerve and use this time to plant native aquatics. Use marginal plants to cover about a third of the pond's surface and plant submerged weeds in the pond for oxygenation. If your pond goes on to develop any large clumps of algae, fish them out with a stick and lay them on the side of the pond for a few days before composting which allows any critters to escape. You will be amazed to find that diving beetles, water boatmen and other small creatures will find your pond on their own. Help to establish the community by begging a bucket of sludge from someone with an established pond.

Once your pond is established, it is easy to be seduced by chemical 'quick fixes' to put right any problems you may experience. Try to resist; there are always organic alternatives.

Water is life's mater and matrix, mother and medium. There is no life without water.

Albert Szent-Gyorgyi, Hungarian Biochemist, 1937 Nobel Prize for Medicine

How did it go?

Q. I need to top up my pond as it has been very hot, and a lot of water has evaporated. Can I use tap water?

A. If you need to top up the pond, use rainwater. Add a diverter and water butt to your downpipes. If you must use tap water, keep it in buckets or tubs for a few days to allow the chlorine to disperse. Chlorine kills aquatic life.

Q. I get clouds of mosquitoes above my pond. Short of spraying them with a bug gun, how can I get rid of them?

A. Don't use a chemical bug spray – it will kill all manner of beneficial insects, and it's not healthy for you, either! Instead, add more floating plants to your pond and add movement, perhaps something like a small solar fountain sprayer, as the water agitation discourages the mosquitoes from breeding. Try to encourage mozzy munchers such as dragonflies by planting appropriately for a breeding colony. Put up bat boxes in your garden as well; they are voracious mosquito eaters.

9. Box clever

Organic box schemes represent quality, locally produced organic food which promotes sustainability and enriches the local economy. It's the ethical ideal.

And you get good value, organic vegetables on your doorstep. Literally.

Veg box, or brown box, schemes were pioneered in the UK by the Soil Association. The idea is simple; people buy organic produce from local producers, fresh from the soil. The scheme helps local producers to find a knowledgeable and consistent market for their crops, which allows them to continue to grow food under organic principles. Under the schemes, the customer knows that food has not been flown or otherwise transported hundreds or thousands of miles before it reaches the kitchen, leaving a large carbon footprint. Food sold as part of a box scheme also allows consumers to munch happily in the knowledge that their food is fresh. The longer the food is stored, the fewer vitamins it contains – and what's the point of eating fruit and vegetables if they are not brimming with goodness?

Seasonality

When I was a girl (cue nostalgic-ad-type music) fruit and vegetables arrived in the shops according to season. Now, I'm not saying I'm never seduced by frozen blueberries from the supermarket in December, but there was real excitement back then when the summer berries started appearing in the greengrocers' shops. You knew that it was summer, and that afternoons were going to be spent making yourself utterly nauseous with a glut of strawberries. As the fruits faded you knew it was nearly time to go back to school… but the pumpkins would soon appear in the shops, glistening with the promise of Halloween. Today, we can buy strawberries, raspberries, blueberries and a myriad of other soft, all-too-perishable fruits all year round in the supermarkets. The rub is, they don't taste of much (they will likely have been picked when unripe and have ripened in storage) and are incredibly expensive. There is a risk that biodiversity will be decreased as some varieties of fruit and vegetables are found to transport more easily than others, causing localised, more diverse varieties to become 'uneconomic' – at least for the supermarkets. As consumers we end up with less choice and a monoculture of tasteless food stacked up in startlingly uniform displays in the bright, antiseptic supermarket environment.

Here's an idea for you…

Check out box schemes near to your home. In the UK, you can find out by looking at the Soil Association's website. You could also try asking your neighbours, some of whom may already be getting boxes (they could give you useful feedback, too), or type 'organic box scheme' into an Internet search engine. The more local the better; you'll be supporting the local economy as well as cutting down on food miles.

Organic box schemes, on the other hand, emphasise the seasonality of foods. Over the summer, they may contain peppers, tomatoes and green beans. In the winter, the emphasis is more squarely set on root vegetables – because that is what is in season in your local area. This aspect of box schemes appeals to many people who like to feel the wheel of the year as it turns, keeping rhythm with the seasons. There is also an element of surprise which is fun. While customers are generally encouraged to specify any vegetables they do not like, there are no guarantees about what will appear from week to week – keeping you out of a rut with your cooking. Children, especially, are interested to see the different veggies appearing and may be tempted to try something new when it appears in the weekly box.

Food miles

Ethical consumers worry about food miles, the journey that the food you buy has taken – possibly having flown miles around the world before you pop it into your shopping trolley. Food miles are responsible for a huge amount of pollution. Food transportation and agriculture accounts for 30% of goods transported by road in the UK alone. The CO_2 emissions from food miles are a major contributor to climate change, and that's without the methane production of farmed animals added to the equation (but that's an argument for vegetarianism rather than organics). In the UK, a report by the Department for the Environment, Food and Rural Affairs (Defra) showed that food miles rose by 15% between 1992 and 2002. Air-freighted food is the worst culprit, contributing an amazing thirty-three times

more CO2 than food eaten in the country where it is produced. Perishable fruits and vegetables are also likely to have been treated with pesticides to prevent spoilage of crops in storage.

In contrast, fruit and vegetables bought under a box scheme are likely to have been grown within fifty miles of your home. That means that, if it comes from the supplier, you have cut down dramatically on food miles and thus on pollution. The food's fresh, the food miles are down: it's a win/win situation!

Far from being a quaint throwback to an earlier time, organic agriculture is proving to be a serious contender in modern farming and a more environmentally sustainable system over the long term.

David Suzuki, geneticist and environmental activist

How did it go?

Q. Our local superstore has a wide range of organic produce. Is it always a bad idea to buy fruit and vegetables from the supermarket?

A. There is no simple equation that says supermarkets equal bad. Don't dismiss the supermarkets as automatically dreadful; many are now stocking locally produced goods. But do look at the labels – where have the fruit and vegetables come from? If the information given is not enough, ask the produce manager in the store. Failing that, email the company involved (it's easy to find their websites online and they all have 'contact us' buttons).

Q. I haven't the time to flit from shop to shop to find everything I need for my family. Can other items be added to a weekly delivery of fruit and vegetables?

A. Many box schemes allow for the addition of other products such as meat, fish, dairy products and even general groceries to your weekly delivery. You can order boxes in different sizes and at different prices – just ask. Most suppliers are very flexible and allow you to create your own weekly delivery.

10. Cuppa chemicals?

Most of us like to start the day with a steaming cup of tea or coffee. But are there dangers lurking in that brew?

As consumers ask more questions about what they are eating and drinking, concerns have been raised about the amount of pesticides contained in the daily cuppa.

Tea, coffee, green tea and herbal tisanes have all been found to be contaminated with pesticide residues, and they're big business.

Trade in coffee alone is worth about $70 billion a year. Coffee production in particular has come in for criticism; pesticides used routinely on coffee plantations include:

- Endosulfan (used against coffee cherry borer): on an environmental level, it is toxic to mammals, birds and fish. It affects the central nervous system, and causes kidney, reproductive system and liver damage. In Columbia, around one hundred poisonings and several deaths each year are directly attributed to poisoning with endosulfan each year.

Here's an idea for you...

Why not have an organic, fair trade coffee week at work to support the charity Coffee Kids, and promote the use of organic tea and coffee as well? Coffee Kids works with coffee farmers' families in Mexico, Guatemala, Nicaragua, Costa Rica and Peru to improve the quality of their lives. It focuses on creating sustainable alternatives that provide income throughout the year, not just during the coffee harvest. The projects supported focus on economic diversification, health care and nutrition, and education.

■ Chlorpyrifos (organophosphate used against coffee cherry borer and coffee leaf miner): toxic to birds, freshwater and marine organisms, and bees. It bioaccumulates and can affect reproduction, being linked to birth defects. In November 2006, the journal *Pediatrics* documented adverse effects on three year olds born to mothers exposed to chlorpyrifos, such as delayed mental development and motor skill impairment.

■ Disulfoton (organophosphate used against leaf miner): very toxic to birds as they eat insects sprayed with the pesticide. Supplied in granular form causing a threat of runoff and contamination of other crops, as coffee is often grown on slopes. Very persistent in the environment; highly toxic to mammals. Causes neurological disorders.

■ Methyl parathion (an organophosphate used against leaf miner): highly toxic. Persists in soil for long periods. Interferes with neurological function. Exposure to high levels may cause dizziness, confusion, headaches, difficult breathing, vomiting, diarrhoea, blurred vision and sweating.

■ Triadimefon (used against coffee rust): accumulates in soil. May cause reproductive problems.

One of the main problems is that although many pesticides have been banned or are strictly regulated in the US or Europe, they remain legal in developing countries, which is where most coffee and tea is grown. This has major ethical implications. Workers in developing countries may not be well informed about dangers in using pesticides, and are less likely to be provided with protective gear than their counterparts in the developed world. Areas where coffee and tea are grown are usually part of complex ecosystems, with high biodiversity, so any environmental damage caused by pesticides and herbicides can have catastrophic effects.

When you buy organic coffee and tea, it will have been produced using sustainable farming practices. Deforestation, for example, is not allowed to occur as part of creating a coffee or tea plantation. Many organic producers embrace Fair Trade ethics, ensuring that the workers on the tea or coffee plantations are not exploited and receive a fair wage for their labour. In addition, many organic coffee producers grow their crop as part of a permaculture system, where coffee is grown alongside food crops such as bananas and avocados, which helps feed the farmers and their families, and is good for biodiversity too.

A lot of the major tea and coffee suppliers now produce organic blends, but you may wish to support smaller companies committed to ethical and organic principles across the board. Search online for information and brands, or check out shops that sell ethical supplies to find a blend that suits you.

Herbal tea

While not strictly tea – it's not produced by the *Camellia sinensis* plant like black and green tea – herbal 'tea' is now a popular alternative. Herbal tea is made from blends of herbs and fruits which are served as an infusion or tisane. Be careful to choose organic blends as these have the best flavour, and you can drink them safe in the knowledge that they are free from potentially harmful pesticides. Some tisanes have specific medicinal properties: for example, peppermint is great for digestion, chamomile soothes and ginger is a good remedy for chills.

Have a go at growing your own blends. Mint is so easy that it becomes invasive in the garden. Plant a clump outside your door – in a pot if you have a small garden – and pick a handful each time you need a soothing brew. Make the fresh herbal tea in a pot and use an old fashioned tea strainer to catch the bits so you avoid 'green teeth syndrome'!

Behind every successful woman is a substantial amount of coffee.

Stephanie Piro, comic artist

How did it go?

Q. I've been drinking green tea for a while now because of all the publicity about its value as an antioxidant, combating free radicals in the body. Now I have seen that lots of green tea contains pesticides. Should I stop drinking it or do the health benefits outweigh the dangers?

A. In some studies pesticide traces have been found in green tea. However, the benefits still probably do outweigh the dangers, with research showing that one cup of green tea has antioxidant effects greater than those provided by a serving of broccoli, spinach, carrots or strawberries. It may be best, though, to play it safe for ultimate health benefits and buy organic. Many blends of organic green tea are available.

Q. I'd like to buy a range of organic herbal teas – but even in my local health store, many blends are not organically certified. Where can I find a supplier?

A. In this case your best bet is probably to do a quick search online; that will throw up many options. A particularly broad range is available from Mountain Rose Herbs. It's also easy to make your own blends by growing herbs organically, either in your garden or in containers. Fresh leaves and flowers make wonderful flavours!

Live organic

11. Dreadful deodorants

Do you slather your armpits in the hope of avoiding an awful odour? You might want to choose carefully. Find out why conventional deodorant reeks.

Substances applied to your skin are absorbed directly into your bloodstream, so is there anything to worry about?

Newspapers and magazines have been full of reports recently about the possible link between deodorants and breast cancer. There have also been reports that the aluminium in deodorants may contribute to Alzheimer's disease. Are these just scare stories?

People produce between one and two pints of sweat a day. It's amazing, with that statistic, that we don't all stink! The thing is, sweat itself is an odourless liquid; it only begins to smell once bacteria begin to break it down. We sweat to regulate temperature, and to excrete toxins dissolved in liquid from our bodies. Many antiperspirants contain products that block the sweat glands, not allowing this excretion to take place. It has been suggested that fatty breast tissue tends to store toxins (as does all fatty tissue), and that antiperspirants can contribute to this. Other studies have suggested that there may be an increase in breast cancer among women using aluminium-based products because the ingredients actually mimic oestrogen – a known contributory factor in the development of

Here's an idea for you...

Tweak your dietary habits to improve your own smell. It has been claimed that eating a lot of meat is a contributory factor in the development of body odour. Try eating lots of leafy green vegetables, sprouted seeds, nuts and whole grains as an alternative to some of your meat dishes and you'll see a difference. It really works! Alcohol and spicy food don't just give you bad breath; you excrete the smell along with toxins through your skin. Cutting down on these types of food will help to cut the likelihood of BO, so a trip to the pub followed by a spicy kebab is out, then! Yoghurt can help, as it affects the bacteria within the body, and try a herbal tea – peppermint and sage can help as well.

breast cancer. A review published in the *Journal of Applied Toxicology* has called for further research to evaluate the potential that this could increase the risk of getting breast cancer.

Concerns have also been raised by a study, published in the *European Journal of Cancer Prevention*, about the fact that the aluminium salts found in antiperspirants and deodorants are applied directly under the arm, adjacent to the breast. If the underarm area is already damaged from shaving, it has been suggested that aluminium may enter the body more readily to affect the lymph nodes nearby.

Here are some ingredients to avoid:

- Aluminium chlorohydrate, aluminium zirconium – or any other aluminium compound. Aluminium can be absorbed through the skin and has been linked to Alzheimer's disease as well as breast cancer
- Parabens – these are derived from tolulene, which is toxic when inhaled, ingested or in contact with the skin. It may cause reproductive disorders
- Triclosan – a skin irritant; may be carcinogenic
- Silica – a skin irritant
- Propylene glycol – absorbed quickly through the skin and enhances penetration of other substances. It's a possible neurotoxin; may cause kidney or liver damage

And now for some gentle alternatives… Well, there are many aluminium-free alternatives to keep you smelling clean and fresh. These work by inhibiting the growth of the bacteria that causes sweat to smell. You can buy a variety of deodorants with ingredients such as lichen, herbal extracts, green tea, aloe vera and essential oils.

The rather literally named Pit-Rok has many devotees. This is a chunk of ammonium alum, a material which has been used cosmetically in Egypt and China for over 2000 years. It works via bacteriostatic action, which means that it inhibits bacterial growth. It allows the excretion of toxins and does not clog pores. You wet the crystal (or use it as you get out of the bath or shower) and rub it in the armpit. It leaves no white marks and doesn't stain clothing. I use it and it seems to work, although it felt weird at first as I was used to feeling something coating my armpit with conventional deodorant. I soon realised it worked just as well, although it left no sticky residue. It's also available as a spray now. Ammonium alum does contain some aluminium, but it is bonded into a molecule that is too large to pass through the skin. Another source of deodorant crystals is Crystal Spring. They really are worth trying, so do some hunting.

Sweat is the cologne of accomplishment.

Stephanie Piro, comic artist

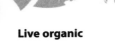

How did it go?

Q. I'd like to try a non-aluminium based deodorant, but I'm worried that they all sound a bit worthy. I want to smell good, and like scented products. Are there any out there?

A. Lots! Try Dr Hauschka skin care's deodorant with neem and sage, or sage and witch hazel. Alternatively, Lavera produce a range of six scents including vervain and lime, and coconut and vanilla. Green People produce a lovely rosemary deodorant with rosemary and lavender essential oils, olive leaf extract and witch hazel. Ask at your local health-food supplier and see what they have in stock, or can order for you.

Q. I suffer from sensitive skin and can react to cosmetic products with rashes and sore, red skin. I'd like to try a crystal mineral deodorant but am worried about the possible effects on my skin. Do you recommend it?

A. Most of the solid crystal deodorant blocks are marketed as hypoallergenic. The only way to be sure is to try a patch test yourself. Try wetting the crystal and stroking it across your wrist. Leave it for twenty-four hours. If you have no reaction, try it on one armpit (you don't want to risk both at once in case you *do* have a reaction and end up doing weird monkey impersonations as you try to scratch). Do not scrub at your armpit with the crystal – just wet and wipe. If you have no reaction after a day, you're home free.

12. Herbal heaven

Fresh herbs at your fingertips – what could be nicer than growing your own in pots or in your garden? Growing them organically, of course!

Read on for the best ways to grow and use your organic herbs.

Whether it's parsley for sauce, mint for tea or echinacea to guard against colds, herbs are one of the most beneficial types of plant you can grow in your garden. Not only do they offer you a battery of flavourings and a handy pharmacopoeia – they also attract beneficial insects such as pollinating bees, and natural pest predators such as ladybirds. By growing your herbs organically, you allow the wildlife that lives in the space to multiply, and they in turn increase the productivity and health of the plants (food or otherwise) that you grow.

Herbs are sturdy plants, and even the most avid pest sprayer would be unlikely to find reason to lather these beauties in chemicals. Many herbs prefer poorer, sandy soils and thrive in unfed soil – so again, those misguided folks with their spray-on fertiliser stay away. Organic gardeners feed and nourish the soil, making it hearty and nutritious with manure (animal or green) and under these conditions, herbs thrive. My herb garden is huge – I admit to being a bit of a herb addict and can't resist visiting herb gardens and nurseries nationwide.

Here's an idea for you...

Don't just dry or freeze your herbs in bags to preserve them. Add a few sprigs to a bottle of olive oil and let the flavours infuse for use in cooking. Or add crumbled leaves to a jar of sea salt to flavour soups and stews. Freeze fresh herb blossoms such as borage, violet or tansy in ice cubes to add to drinks. With a little imagination, you'll think of many more ideas!

My own herbs are growing in less than perfect conditions on a heavy clay soil – they mainly prefer well-drained conditions. But with the help of manure from the horses, and Sweetpea the goat, the soil is regularly fed and broken down. Organic manure dug in during the autumn also helps to aerate the soil as it improves the texture. Dig in some horticultural grit to open up the soil as most herbs hate having 'wet feet'. You can make this easier by building a small raised bed for your herbs. I made mine from slabwood, and they look just the part. Slabwood is the 'trimming' left behind when a tree trunk is cut to make planks. It still has the bark attached so looks very rustic. Even better, they virtually give it away at the sawmills. A bundle of fifty pieces bought in 2007 cost me £10. Make the bed by hammering foot long pegs made from 5 cm x 5 cm timber into the ground. Then nail the slabwood to the pegs to make a box shape – and fill with your soil and grit.

Organic herbs seem to me to have a cleaner, stronger flavour. When you use the herbs to flavour your food, you are adding no chemicals and they are thus so much healthier to consume than artificial 'flavourings' full of E numbers and additives from a test tube. You can grow herbs in pots on the windowsill or yard as well as in the garden. If your space is limited, choose carefully. You do not have to grow the obvious herbs such as chives or parsley (unless they are favourites, of course). Be adventurous. Not only will you discover new tastes, but you will save money as more unusual herbs can be expensive to buy – especially organic versions. Try growing sorrel, to give salads and sauces a sharp, refreshing taste, or try chervil for adding to scrambled eggs or omelettes. Visit a herb supplier or garden and investigate the herbs that appeal to you. There may be all sorts of wonders out there that you have not discovered yet.

There is no kind of herb, but somebody or other says that it is good. I am very glad to hear it.

Henry David Thoreau, author and philosopher

How did it go?

Q. I want to use more organic herbs in my cooking, and I like making bath preparations. I live in a flat, though, and can't grow enough for my needs in pots. Where can I get good quality organic herbs without breaking the bank?

A. Ask your friends with gardens if they have any herbs they can spare, as they may have a lot of something like rosemary or lemon balm, and search online (check out Organic Herb Trading, for instance). Another thing you might like to do is make friends with the people who run your local health-food shop. They may well buy dried herbs in bulk, quite likely from a wholesaler who supplies organic goods, so you could come to a reasonable agreement about price and larger quantities. You won't know if you don't ask!

Q. I don't want to dabble about in things I don't know enough about – it could be dangerous. How do I know if herbs are safe to eat if I buy them as plants and use them myself?

A. Invest in a good book – or several – and get reading. Most of the herbs safe to use in cookery are very easy to identify. Buy your herb plants from a reputable supplier who grows herbs according to organic principles, either in person or by mail order, and you know exactly what it is you are getting. Learn the Latin names for the plants – not as hard as it sounds – as there is less room for error when you are reading and comparing different books. Good suppliers will often give you factsheets or advice, too. If you fancy using herbal remedies, be cautious. They are wonderful, but you should seek professional advice as dosage is as important – and as potentially dangerous – as with conventional drugs.

13. Milk matters – organic dairy products

Milk and dairy products seem like some of the most naturally good-for-you foods, just as they come. So why should we bother with organic versions?

Here's why the white stuff is not always the right stuff.

It's not rocket science. If cows are treated with pesticides, and graze on fields treated with pesticides and herbicides, some of the chemicals enter their bodies. When they give milk, that milk contains low levels of pesticide residues. When we drink it, it enters our bodies and is stored in our body fat. Dairy cows are also treated with drugs to increase milk yields and keep them free from possible disease.

The USDA (United States Department for Agriculture) runs a pesticide data programme, which tests for pesticide residue in foods. In 1998, it tested milk and dairy produce. It found relatively low levels of residue, mainly DDE, a breakdown product of the insecticide DDT. Alarmingly, this was banned in the US in the 1970s so it shows how persistent the chemical is in the soil if traces were still being found a decade later!

Try upping your intake of milk – organic of course, with all those extra nutrients – by making fruity milkshakes. Don't put the blender away when you've finished; it's too easy to forget it's there. Keep it out in clear view in the kitchen. When you've used it, take a tip from the juice bars and swoosh a jug full of water through to clean it – or you'll have another excuse not to use it as it will be full of rotting fruit pulp. Go one step further and freeze the shakes to make delicious organic ice cream.

In February 2006, the results of testing in 2004 were released. Every milk sample tested (739) had pesticide residue. DDE was found in 96% of samples, and diphenylamine was found in 98% of the samples. This is an industrial chemical used in the manufacture of rubber and plastic as well as being used as an apple tree growth regulator (what happened to just planting apple trees and letting them grow?). DPA is also sprayed on apples which are stored to delay ripening. Possibly, the cows tested were fed apple waste; DPA may also have entered the food chain when used as an animal drug, or even via rubber and plastics used in milk production and storage. Dieldrin (an insecticide), pyrethroid insecticide and endosulfan, which has been found to disrupt endocrine function, were also found.

These worrying findings must be viewed in perspective – these are actually low levels of pesticides. However, milk is a very important part of the diet of small children, who are particularly vulnerable to the effects of toxins as their bodies grow and develop.

Perhaps buying organic milk and dairy products such as cheese and yoghurts is a way to play it safe. Organically certified dairy farmers use only organic fertilisers on their land and treat any pests with organically approved measures. They do not give their cows supplemental hormones, to boost milk production, or bovine growth hormone. The cows are fed organically and are not given GM cattle feed. From an animal welfare point of view, organic dairy farming is more humane. Organic systems involving rotation and leaving fields to 'rest' tends to mean that cows have richer pasture and larger areas to graze than conventionally reared cows. Finally, during processing, organically certified milk is protected from further chemical contamination.

Organic milk – better nutritionally?

Recent research presented to the Soil Association's annual conference in 2005 suggested that organic milk has higher levels of vitamin E, omega-3 fatty acids (also found in oily fish, which are believed to help provide protection from heart disease) and antioxidants. Specifically, the study found that organic milk had around 50% higher levels of vitamin E than conventionally produced milk and was also found to have 75% higher levels of beta carotene, also found in orange and yellow vegetables. Amazingly, it also contained two to three times more of the antioxidants lutein and zeaxanthine than regular milk. Antioxidants help your body to protect itself from damaging free radicals caused by pollution and toxins, so it has to be worth making the change.

I asked the waiter, 'Is this milk fresh?' He said, 'Lady, three hours ago it was grass.'
Phyllis Diller, comedienne

How did it go?

Q. Why does organic milk cost more than other milk? Isn't it just another way of saying 'this is a premium product – expect to pay more'?

A. As with other organically produced foods, it is costly for dairy farmers to follow the government standards that are required to become certified as organic producers, farmers who are legally permitted to label their food as such. As organic farming methods become more widespread, the price differential may well decrease. While organic milk is a premium product, containing more nutrients than conventional milk, many people are prepared to pay the difference not just for health reasons but also for taste.

Q. I've heard that even major fast food chains are starting to stock organic milk to pull in families! Isn't organic milk just a bit of a fad?

A. Well, organic food is entering the mainstream as more people become informed about the quality and safety of foods they eat. It's true that McDonalds has announced that it's switching to organic milk for its coffee and hot chocolate drinks – but this is a good thing. While they may or may not have introduced the milk as a marketing exercise (when they announced that their coffee beans were to be bought solely from sources certified by the conservation group the Rainforest Alliance sales rose by 10%), their customers also benefit.

14. Green goddess

With increasing public concern about dioxins in sanitary products, many women are looking for alternatives. How easy is it to find something fitting the 'green' bill which is comfy, secure and convenient?

From organic cotton pads to Mooncups — here are some greener solutions.

First on the green agenda is the issue of where all the discarded sanitary towels, tampons and nauseatingly titled panty liners (frankly, I wear knickers and wouldn't know a pair of panties if they leapt up and bit me) go when they are flushed or discarded. Landfill is increasingly full of them, and they take a l-o-n-g time to biodegrade, with their often plastic backings, and beaches are swamped with them. More than four million tampons and pads are flushed every day in the UK alone, where women buy more than three billion disposable sanitary products every year. A Western woman will use around 12,000 tampons or sanitary towels in her lifetime. That's a lot of waste.

Second – but just as important – there's the question of whether the products that we use to mop up our monthlies are actually safe to use. Tampons are usually made from cotton or rayon, and rayon is made from chemically processed wood pulp. Disposable pads and liners are also sometimes made from wood

There are reusable devices, such as a Keeper (rubber) or a Mooncup (silicone), designed to be inserted into your vagina like a contraceptive cap. These catch menstrual blood and are rinsed out regularly. Lots of women first come across them when looking for something convenient to use when backpacking, and they're very 'green'; they can last for years if you look after them.

pulp, bleached from natural brown to dazzling white. Until recently, elemental chlorine was used – and this was a source of dioxin which is a known carcinogen. Dioxin builds up cumulatively in the body over time, right from the moment we are born. After campaigns from such groups as the Women's Environmental Network (WEN) manufacturers have moved onto chlorine dioxide or hydrogen peroxide. Think about it though: do these items really need to be white? They are just destined to get messed up anyway. Would it matter if they came out of the packet unbleached?

If we think about the cotton used in the production of sanitary products we meet another dilemma. Cotton production accounts for 10% of the pesticide used in the world today. That means the growers suffer health problems as a result of exposure, and the pesticide is detrimental to wildlife. In addition to this, pesticide residues are found in the cotton produced. Think about this too – your vagina walls are very thin and the mucous membrane remains damp to protect the body from infection. Add a tampon potentially contaminated with pesticide residue and some of that residue may find its way through the damp mucous membrane into the body. There is also, of course, the potential risk from Toxic Shock Syndrome (TSS). This is rare but fatal, and strikes quickly. It has been linked to super-absorbent rayon tampons (rather than 100% cotton) which may encourage the growth of the bacteria staphylococcus aureus.

Now, we all know the adage that you should never put anything in your vagina that you would not put in your mouth. Even with pads, residues such as pesticides and dioxins from the bleaching process are held next to your skin and these chemicals have been linked to birth defects, reproductive disorders and cancer. Perhaps we should think harder about the risks we take with our bodies when we choose our sanitary protection, in the same way as we think about the food we put into our mouths. And many women suffer unnecessarily from irritation and rashes due to perfumes added to sanitary protection. Nobody wants to smell, but a daily bath would have the same effect. A worrying development has been the introduction of tampons with added lubricants which contain parabens; these chemicals are suspected of being oestrogen mimics which can damage fertility. Some towels contain super-absorbent polyacrylate gel which absorbs moisture. There is a possible danger with these super absorbencies that women will change less regularly and that dangerous levels of bacteria may develop.

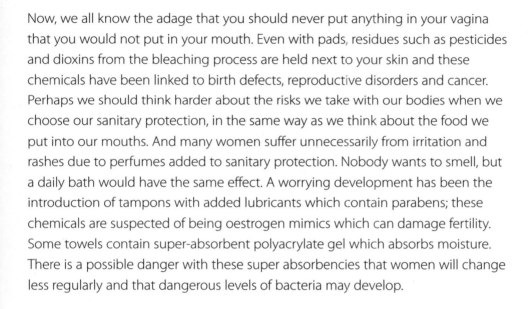

If women are supposed to be less rational and more emotional at the beginning of our menstrual cycle when the female hormone is at its lowest level, then why isn't it logical to say that, in those few days, women behave the most like the way men behave all month long?

Gloria Steinem, campaigner

So what can you do about it? Well, sanitary products containing unbleached, organic cotton are available. You could also consider using washable cotton pads and even make them yourself; the Women's Environmental Network provide a pattern on their website. You won't be alone; in 1983, a World Health Organisation survey of women in ten countries around the world found that more than 45% used home-made pads – so finding this idea strange could be a cultural taboo. It seem may like a weird idea, but look at the number of parents turning to washable nappies instead of disposables; nobody thinks that's weird.

How did it go?

Q. *I wouldn't mind giving washable pads a try, but I'm not keen on making my own. Where can I find out more?*

A. A good place to start could be your local health-food shop; they might stock them anyway or have access to a wholesaler who does. Failing that, go online and try to find a local supplier. Check out Luna Pads and Glad Rags for details of commercially available reusable pads; even if they're not convenient suppliers for you, you'll get a good idea of what you're looking for.

Q. *All very scary... what are the symptoms of TSS and how can I avoid it?*

A. Like severe flu – sudden high fever, vomiting, diarrhoea, feeling faint/dizzy, confusion, muscle aches, a sunburn-like rash – but it can be treated if diagnosed early, so seek medical advice if these symptoms are present. Use organic tampons with the lowest absorbency possible and use a sanitary towel for some of the time – maybe at night. Change tampons regularly with clean hands (wash them before changing as well as after).

15. Hidden dangers

In the organic kitchen the utensils and pans you use can be just as important as the ingredients in terms of health.

It's not enough to consider the food you eat — now you have to think about the safety of the items you use in the kitchen during food preparation as well.

It seems from recent research that chemicals may leach out of cookware, pans and utensils as you use them, contaminating food. There's no point in lovingly growing and preparing great organic food if you spoil it at the last hurdle!

Aluminium
There have been a lot of scare stories in the press about aluminium and the links it has with Alzheimer's disease. In the 1970s it was discovered that Alzheimer's sufferers had high levels of aluminium in their brain tissue. It was not clear as to whether this was a potential cause of the disease, or a result. It was suggested

that it might be wise to discard aluminium pans and kettles and many people did just that. It is worth noting, however, that aluminium is present in large amounts in the environment – it is the third commonest element in the earth's crust, after oxygen and silicon, and is present in the air, soil and water. Also, if you take certain medications, you are exposing yourself to a high intake of aluminium. Many antacids, for example, contain high concentrations of aluminium; one tablet can contain more than 50 mg and aspirin may contain 10 to 20 mg. A person using uncoated aluminium pans is likely to ingest up to 3.5 mg daily. Really, it comes down to making your own informed decisions. If you use aluminium cookware, don't cook or store highly acidic or salty foods such as tomato sauces, rhubarb, citrus, etc., as this might allow more aluminium than usual to enter your food.

Here's an idea for you...

Consider trying out cast iron pans. They have not been implicated in health risks and it has even been suggested that they may add iron to your diet! Cast iron pans are great for cooking stews and soups as they heat evenly and retain heat well, meaning that they can be used at relatively low temperatures. They are great for simmering food, and I have found that food does not readily stick or burn. The pans are heavy, even when empty – but they look great enough to serve food from them at the table.

Teflon

Teflon cookware is convenient, non-stick and useful – but is it safe? It has been claimed that using a Teflon pan may cause health problems if the pan is heated to too high a temperature. Scientists at the University of Toronto found that Teflon breaks down into neurotoxins and greenhouse gases at high temperatures. If heated to over 360ºC, it gives off fumes. These may cause flu-like symptoms such as chills, fever and headaches, and scientists have dubbed this 'polymer-fume fever'. While pans are not routinely used at these temperatures, they could occur where food is boiled dry or burned. Tests conducted in the US on Teflon cookware have found that they heat to higher than the danger point within two to five minutes on a high setting on a conventional cooker. A Teflon pan reached 382ºC in five minutes.

In a recent review of Teflon's safety in the US, the Environmental Protection Agency (EPA) recommended that perfluorochemicals (PFC) – a chemical given off by overheated Teflon – should be described as a likely carcinogen. PFCs do not biodegrade and they accumulate in body tissue and they have been shown in laboratory tests to be toxic to mammals. Heated to temperatures consistent with everyday cooking, Teflon emits minute particles that can lodge deeply in the lungs. These particles are deadly to pet birds and can cause polymer-fume fever in humans. PFCs have been shown to accumulate in organs like the liver, gall bladder and thyroid gland. They may also impair immune function.

If you want to avoid Teflon, consider using stainless steel, cast iron, Pyrex or silicone cookware. In addition, check for Teflon coatings on clothing and furnishings. Be wary of fast food packaging, which often contains PFCs, and cosmetics and creams that contain PTFE in ingredient lists.

Copper

Copper pans look wonderful, and are excellent for making delicate sauces as copper conducts heat very evenly. Many top chefs use copper kitchenware. Be careful though; most copper cookware is lined with stainless steel or even tin – and this is for a reason. Copper is fairly easily dissolved by some foods (particularly acidic ones) and if it enters food it can cause nausea and vomiting.

Plastics

Many ready meals are sold in plastic containers, ready for microwaving or popping in the oven. There has been some concern about chemicals from the plastic migrating into the heated food – especially with fatty or sugary food. To play it safe, empty food into Pyrex dishes (or similar) beforehand. On a similar note, avoid wrapping fatty foods such as butter or cheese in plastic film for storage as plastics may migrate more easily into fatty foods.

Good kitchen equipment is expensive, but most items last a lifetime and will pay for themselves over and over again.

Delia Smith, TV cook

How did it go?

Q. I got a silicone muffin pan for Christmas. Is it really safe to use plastic in the oven?

A. Silicone may look like plastic – but it isn't. It is a type of synthetic rubber. It contains bonded silicone – a natural element found in many rocks and sand. Food-grade silicone is very safe, and there is no known health risk associated with its use. It does not react with food and does not emit any fumes. However, don't use silicone above 220°C as it starts to melt. It's hard wearing and easy to use, so give it a go!

Q. Can I reheat food I have frozen in margarine tubs, etc., in the microwave?

A. No, never use 'recycled' pots such as these in your microwave. They have not been heat tested for this use and may allow chemicals to leach into food. On the same note, always remove meat or fish from butcher trays and wraps before microwave defrosting.

Live organic

70

16. Gaia's garden

'Organic gardening' sounds very lofty and as though it takes a lot of thought and effort. In reality, there are just a few principles to stick to in order to reap the benefits.

So how do you go about creating your own organic garden?

My dad is in his eighties. He has always been an organic gardener – he just doesn't call it that. My parents' allotments were always bursting with delicious edibles (and a few cutting flowers for the house) that had never had a whiff of a chemical. Why? Firstly, because it was cheaper. Secondly, they used 'good husbandry' techniques that avoided many pest problems. They kept an eye on their crops and nipped any problems in the bud. A daily 'tour of duty' enabled plants to be checked, food to be harvested and any plants under glass to be watered. It also allowed him time for a quick puff on a stinky pipe that smelled as though he was setting fire to the compost heap, but that's another story!

I garden organically. I am far more pompous about it than my parents, but I have absorbed most of their ideas (I passed when it came to the pipe habit, though). My first priority – and the priority of organic gardeners the world over – is my soil. This black gold is priceless. Improve your soil constantly. Add leaf mould, garden compost and manure. Make your compost heap the hub of your garden. I made the mistake of making my first efforts too far from the house, so make sure yours

71

Here's an idea for you...

Have a go at trench composting. I have found that it is best started in the autumn to give the waste time to rot, weather and settle before planting in the spring. Dig a trench a spade wide and deep – make it as long as you need. Pile the soil by the trench as you will need it soon. Drop kitchen waste such as peelings into the trench and cover them with a thin layer of soil. This helps the waste to be exposed to a large number of micro-organisms to speed rotting. Alternate layers of waste and soil until the trench is full. This sort of trench is a brilliant place to grow greedy feeders such as runner beans and peas.

is within convenient slipper-clad-feet distance or you are less likely to add things to it. These should be organic veggie and fruit peelings (go steady with citrus), tea leaves, clippings from the garden, lawn clippings, hair from hairbrushes, egg shells, etc. Your compost bin is the engine that drives the garden. In parts of my garden, the soil is so rich and crumbly that it looks distinctly edible, like cocoa powder. It is very much a case of only getting out what you put in, so make sure your soil is well cared for and nurtured.

When your soil is fed well, it encourages the tiny organisms and larger soil-dwelling friends such as earthworms. These help to create a favourable environment for your plants to grow, as well as benefiting the environment as a whole as wildlife is encouraged into your garden to feed on these edible beasties. If your garden is free from heavy-duty chemicals, the natural predators of baddies such as slugs and aphids come roaring into the garden for a feast. Hedgehogs and birds deal with snails, leatherjackets and slugs, and battalions of creatures including ladybirds and lacewings will despatch aphids. Make sure you encourage this beneficial wildlife by adding rock and log piles, and adding bundles of hollow stems to wilder areas for ladybirds and lacewings to overwinter ('ladybird hotels' look fabulous but are an unnecessary expense where money is tight). Make sure you pull weeds when they are small, so they do not leach goodness from the soil, and add a mulch to help keep their numbers down.

Choose disease-resistant varieties of plant seed wherever possible; they are usually described as such in the catalogues. This can give your plants a head start. Make sure seedlings are well-watered and never allowed to become leggy as they strain for light. If they become stressed, plants are prone to disease. Another important concept to accept is imperfection. We have all become used to our carrots, potatoes and tomatoes looking uniform and unblemished. In reality, this usually means that lots of fertiliser and pesticide has been used, and many tonnes of fruit and vegetables have been pulped because they were not 'perfect'. By growing your own organically, you reject these 'factory farming' methods and grow for taste and goodness rather than appearance. It can lead to some great laughs, as well, as you eat a tomato that has grown into the shape of your Aunt Dot or a carrot that has grown legs and looks like a mandrake…

The more simple we are, the more complete we become.

Auguste Rodin

How did it go?

Q. I usually like to have a good bonfire to get rid of my garden waste. Is that still OK in an organic garden?

A. Organic gardening goes hand in hand with conservation and care of the environment – and don't forget that bonfires can add to background air pollution. I tend to compost as much as I can (shredding if necessary) and only burn diseased material. Give it a try; it's a shame to lose all those resources for the compost heap by burning them!

Q. I'd like to grow organic food but am not very good at remembering to plant seeds at the right time. I buy plug plants for flowers. Can I do the same for organic vegetables?

A. Well, an increasing number of gardening centres are carrying a small range of young organic vegetable plants. Your best bet, however is still to buy by mail order. Rocket Gardens in the UK has an excellent range and even takes the stress out of choosing with whole veggie plot boxes – do some research to find a local supplier who does something similar if necessary.

17. Organic ornamentals

You may not have thought about it, but that beautiful bouquet from the florist may not be so green – and can even have harmful effects on the environment and your health…

Organic bouquets and potted plants? If you're not going to eat it, why should it be organic?

During the last two years the interest in organic flowers has grown immensely. At first glance, this could just seem faddy. But think about it: if we are consumers of organic goods, we care about our health and the health of the environment. Conventionally produced cut flowers and ornamental plants are laced with pesticides and herbicides, and are usually grown with chemical fertilisers. Obviously, this is not good for the environment. Many cut flowers and plants are sprayed with toxic chemicals to make them cosmetically perfect and to make them last. These chemicals then enter our homes on the innocent-looking bouquet or potted plant.

You bring flowers into your home to beautify it, to make your home welcoming and restful. If they are organic, you will feel safe to touch and smell the blooms and enjoy their sensual pleasures without worrying about chemical overload. Another benefit of organic cut flowers is that they last longer. They way in which organic flowers are grown, as the produce of strong, well-nourished plants, ensures that they are hardy and their 'vase life' is longer.

Here's an idea for you...

Why not grow some flowers and herbs to dry for arrangements all year round? Choose plants for their seed pods as well as their flowers and foliage. For pods, choose nigella (love-in-a-mist), quaking grass, artichoke, teasel, poppy, fennel, Iris foetidissima (with its wonderful common name of 'stinking gladwyn'), honesty, phalaris, millet, corn, barley. For dried flowers, go for hops, lavender, achillea (yarrow), cornflowers, roses, globe thistles, Helichrysum (straw flower), statice, hydrangea. It is also worth sowing a packet of ornamental gourds for drying. If you varnish them they will keep their colour for a long time and look attractive in a basket. They are great Halloween decorations, too!

In addition, many of the more exotic blooms are produced in developing countries where the methods of the flower farms – intensive production and land clearance – are questionable, and the treatment of workers often unethical. They are more likely to work under unsafe conditions, and to be exposed to dangerous chemicals which cause dermatitis and breathing problems.

Grow your own

Cut flowers – and especially organic bouquets – are lovely, but they are sometimes expensive. Why not have a go at growing your own cutting garden? Choose a patch of the garden that gets full sun for most of the day. Make sure you dig in lots of organic matter so the ground is well fed and drains freely. If your soil is heavy clay or otherwise difficult, make a raised bed for your cutting garden as this will radically improve drainage. Make sure the cutting garden is well sheltered. Planting a strip of wheat along the edge of the area not only makes a quick-growing windbreak; you can also harvest it in the autumn for seasonal displays. A row of sweet peas grown up a simple frame will also help to act as a windbreak – and will provide fragrant, colourful flowers.

I like to grow many perennials in my cutting garden. Peonies, for example, make wonderful opulent vases of blowsy colour. Roses are an obvious but no less

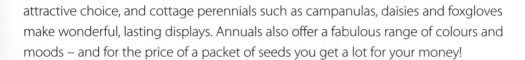

attractive choice, and cottage perennials such as campanulas, daisies and foxgloves make wonderful, lasting displays. Annuals also offer a fabulous range of colours and moods – and for the price of a packet of seeds you get a lot for your money!

A bed that is 2 m by 3 m will give most people a large enough area to produce cutting annuals for a season. Add perennials, herbs and evergreen foliage as well as berried shrubs and you will have cut flowers all year round. Many annuals are multi-stemmed and repeat flower all season. In fact, cutting the flowers will encourage the plants to bloom again.

Flowers for cutting
Your choice will obviously be influenced by your tastes, but you may want to consider the following: sunflowers (including dark russet coloured and fluffy 'teddy bear' varieties), snapdragons, larkspur, cosmos, globe amaranth, zinnias, pinks, anemones, gypsophila, nicotiana, asters, delphinium, dahlias, chrysanthemums, echinacea, Michaelmas daisies and shirley poppies. When you are thinking about greenery and foliage, consider asparagus fern, and herbs such as rosemary, sage (including variegated), lavender and mint. Just look in any organic seed catalogue and you will be spoilt for choice!

A bit of fragrance clings to the hand that gives flowers.

Chinese proverb

How did it go?

Q. I keep seeing labels on cut flowers that say 'VeriFlora' and 'wildcrafted'. What do these labels mean? Are they a good thing?

A. VeriFlora is; it's an American sustainability certification programme that applies to cut flowers and potted plants. If your flowers are labelled VeriFlora, this guarantees that they have been grown in an environmentally friendly and socially responsible manner. Wildcrafted is a slightly more controversial label. Wildcrafted plants have been harvested from their natural habitat. You may see this label on some seed pods, sea vegetables, wild rice and herbs. In the US, Wildcrafted plants are regulated by the Organic Food Production Act of 1991. Under the Act, harvesters must define the area they are harvesting and must show that the harvest will sustain the wild crop. The gathering is carried out in a sustainable way, with branches, berries and flowers taken and the base plant left behind to recover. If the whole plant is taken, seeds are planted in the empty hole.

Q. Why are organic flowers significantly more expensive than non-organic? Is it just because people will pay more for premium products?

A. There are several reasons. Organic methods are more labour-intensive than conventional methods, and therefore tend to be more costly in terms of 'person hours'. The yield can tend to be lower, and the flowers take slightly longer to mature. All this adds on to the end price – but for the gains in fragrance and the lack of noxious chemicals, it's worth it.

18. Get fruity!

Grow your own fruit – in pots, indoors or in mixed organically gardened beds, there's something for everyone.

Fruit, especially soft summer berries, can often be one of the most expensive items on the organic shopping list — but it's incredibly easy to grow.

Probably the main thing I grow here on our organic smallholding is fruit. From bush fruits such as blackcurrants and redcurrants to soft fruits such as strawberries and raspberries, we have it all. Three years ago I planted up my smallest field as an orchard with apples, plums, greengages, cherries and pears. I didn't forget the all-important crab apples for making jelly. Combined with exotics such as Japanese wine berries and many varieties of blackberry hybrids such as tayberries, we are well fruited… I also had a huge crop of peaches this year, grown in my polytunnel. I don't tell you all this to boast – although I am smug – but to show what is possible. Organic fruit tastes better, obviously has the health benefits associated with a lack of pesticides – and growing your own is really cheap. The air miles associated are great too…

In the garden
Even one apple tree and one plum tree in a garden bed, underplanted with blackcurrant and redcurrant bushes, will give you a large amount of fruit. Add

Make your own organic liquid feed for next to nothing. Manure soup sounds foul but fruit plants, especially, love it. Fill a hessian bag or old tights with horse manure. Fresh is fine; it doesn't have to be rotted. Suspend the bag in a bucket of water and leave to percolate for a week or two. The resulting soup can be added to watering cans at a concentration of about one part to ten of water. Alternatively crush a handful of comfrey leaves into a hessian bag/tights, adding seaweed if you have any. This can be suspended in water again in the same way as the manure. Use it, also diluted, to feed the soil.

blackberries and hazel to a hedge to make it productive. Just be prepared to think creatively about planting schemes. Fruit trees adapt to the room made available. Most trees bought now are on dwarfing or semi-dwarfing rootstock, so they will not overpower your garden. To avoid a disappointing fruit crop, make sure that you check the pollination needs of the type of fruit you choose to grow. If it isn't self-pollinating you will need to grow more than one plant of the same type, or a cross pollinator, in order to see fruit.

The best way to integrate fruit into your garden is to embrace forest gardening. This system plans gardens in terms of layers, modelled on a natural forest. It uses fruit and nut trees and bushes, herbs and vegetables to create a layered, naturalistic garden. I have areas of my smallholding (including increasing areas in the orchard) planned in this way and intend to increase it. It is easier to maintain than a conventional bed system and looks great. It would be easy to use an area of your garden in this way either in a corner or as an island bed. The system makes companion planting particularly easy and encourages beneficial insects.

In the yard or on the patio

If you just have a yard or patio, you can still have a fruit tree. Plant dwarfing rootstock fruit trees in half-barrels and they will thrive. When growing these in pots, you need to make especially sure that the soil is well nourished, so add plenty of organic feed. Containers also make it easier to grow tender plants which may not overwinter well outside. Strawberries grow well in containers as long as they are well fed. I have several varieties of strawberries, including tiny sweet alpine strawberries, growing in half-barrels on the patio as we have rapacious field slugs that like nothing better than a juicy strawberry to munch on. The barrels raise the berries up as they ripen so they are less vulnerable. As they ripen, it is also worth covering them with sheer fleece to protect them from hungry birds.

The key to growing in containers is to monitor watering. For most plants, the surface of the soil should be allowed to become dry to the touch before watering. Overwatering causes more deaths than underwatering, as plants rot. Good drainage of excess water is essential, so make sure you put plenty of broken crocks, pebbles or shingle in the bottom of the pot before adding organic compost. Those horrible polystyrene packaging chips finally have a use: add them as a light drainage medium. They are great if you ever need to move the containers (i.e. in and out of the house seasonally) as they are obviously a lot lighter than broken crocks or pebbles!

One that would have the fruit must climb the tree.

Thomas Fuller, physician, preacher and intellectual

How did it go?

Q. I'd like to grow blueberries as they are delicious and full of antioxidants, but expensive. I've heard that they can be difficult. Any tips?

A. They need acidic soil, so get a testing kit and check your garden. Otherwise, you need to grow them in organic ericaceous compost, in a container or a raised bed. If you do this, monitor the soil's pH every few years as it may be necessary to add acid. Give the plants a high-potash feed in the growing season, mulch them with pine needles or wood chips and use water from the water butt – all these will help to keep the soil acidic enough. Finally, plant two different varieties if you can – if you have more than one, the yields are higher and the berries are bigger.

Q. Which plants are good for growing in pots?

A. Well, they most obviously include apples, pears, plums and cherries. Apricots, citrus, nectarines and peaches can also be grown in pots and brought inside over the winter if necessary. Most soft fruits such as strawberries, blueberries, currants, gooseberries and grapes are also suitable for growing in containers. Blackberries and their hybrids don't thrive in pots, though, because they are naturally vigorous and need space to spread.

19. Terrific teeth

Dental care products can be full of all sorts of chemicals – so why not try organic alternatives?

Read on to discover the toothpaste ingredients that might wipe the smile off your face...

Toothpaste keeps us free from cavities, gives us whiter teeth and fresher breath. Watch any toothpaste advertisement and you will be baffled by the science flung at you left, right and centre about amazing new ingredients. What could be bad about that? Well, the chemicals used to maintain this cosmetic dream can be very dangerous. Many of the big-brand toothpastes and mouthwashes contain potentially harmful ingredients. These ingredients have small molecules that can penetrate the tissue of your mouth and enter your bloodstream. This is especially the case when gums bleed as your teeth are brushed. So what are these ingredients that you may wish to avoid?

- **Sodium fluoride**. This has been recommended for generations to prevent cavities. It does that job, but the benefits have to be weighed against the possible dangers. Fluoride can, in large doses, cause muscular weakness and convulsions, respiratory distress and cardiac failure. Have you seen the warnings on some toothpastes to say that they should only be used by

Make your own organic mouthwash. Stir into a cup of water a quarter of a teaspoon of baking soda, a drop of organic peppermint oil, and a drop of organic tea-tree oil. Pour this into a clean jar and shake to blend; use as required. The tea-tree oil acts as an antiseptic and helps to fight gum disease and the bacteria that causes bad breath and plaque. Another alternative is a rosemary mouthwash. Boil two cups of water, adding a sprig of fresh mint, a sprig of rosemary (best crushed) and a teaspoon of anise seeds. It smells delicious as it heats; when it is cool, strain and use as necessary.

children aged six and above? A dose of toothpaste a bit more than 100 g – if a toddler chews on a tube, for example – can kill a young child in two to four hours. Sodium fluoride is used in insecticides and rat poisons, and acts as a neurotoxin. Tests have shown that fluoride enhances the brain's propensity for absorbing aluminium, which has been linked with Alzheimer's disease. In studies of osteoporosis, fluoride has also been linked to the development of limited joint mobility, ligament calcification and muscular degeneration.

- **Sodium lauryl sulphate (SLS)** is added to toothpaste because it foams. It's a gimmick rather than a necessary cleanser; people feel that the toothpaste is working if it foams up. SLS has been found to be an irritant and can act corrosively on skin tissue. The journal of the American College of Toxicology has reported that SLS can penetrate and be retained in the eye, brain, heart and liver. In the cleaning industry, SLS is used as a strong degreaser, in garage floor cleaners, used on engines and in car-wash soaps. Just how dirty do you think those teeth of yours are?

- **Triclosan**. Not so long ago, toothpastes using triclosan emblazoned its use across the wrapper as though it were a miracle cure. Recent studies are casting new light on this ingredient, however. Researchers have found that triclosan can react with the chlorine found in tap water to make chloroform! This is a highly toxic, carcinogenic chemical; if you breathe enough chloroform it can be fatal. So, you rinse your toothbrush in water, add toothpaste and brush – facilitating a nice little chemical reaction in your mouth.

Of course, the chemicals in the toothpaste aren't just bad for you – they're bad for the environment. Every time we spit after brushing, the chemicals are washed down the drain. These harmful chemicals persist in the aquatic environment where they can build up in the bodies of wildlife. They can also come back to bite us in our drinking water supply.

Greener alternatives

Luckily, there are many safer alternatives on the market. Search the Internet for companies like Green People, who sell toothpastes made with organic essential oils, myrrh and vitamin C to protect against bacterial growth – the main cause of gum disease. They also sell a mouthwash containing cloves, cinnamon and myrrh. Health-food shops often carry 'green' toothpastes.

As a complete alternative to traditional brushing, try a natural toothbrush. It's a traditional method of cleaning teeth, using a root from the araak tree (*Saladora persica*). It massages the teeth and gums and prevents the formation of cavities. It is widely used in the Middle East. The root contains silicon, vitamin C and minerals that strengthen and whiten tooth enamel such as potassium, sodium, chloride, sodium bicarbonate and calcium oxide.

Another alternative is a new type of high-tech toothbrush developed in Japan, called Soladey. It looks like any other ordinary toothbrush, but has a metal rod running through the replaceable bristle head into the handle. The photosensitive titanium rod is activated by light (sun or indoor light) to produce negatively charged electrons that help to remove plaque from your teeth. These blend with saliva to attract positive (hydrogen) ions from the acid in your dental plaque. Acid is neutralised and plaque broken down – without a hint of toothpaste! The handle and rod last for years; the heads are replaceable.

A smile is a curve that sets everything straight.

Phyllis Diller, comedienne

How did it go?

Q. I like using tooth-whitening products, but I am concerned about the safety of the chemicals they contain. Are there any organic options available?

A. There are many on the market. One is Spirit of Nature's tooth whitener, containing kaolin, silica, calcium carbonate and peppermint. You brush your teeth with the powder once a day for a bright smile.

Q. My regular dental floss has added fluoride. Are non-fluoridated versions as efficient?

A. Absolutely. Floss is made to get rid of tiny particles trapped between teeth. Whether it is fluoridated or not, it will do the job; the choice is yours. There are many options available including varieties made from silk and coated in beeswax and essential oils. Check your local wholefood supplier.

20. Here comes the sun

We've all taken on board the message about protecting our skin from the sun. But just how safe is the sun cream we're using?

Everybody knows that sunscreen should be used to avoid premature ageing, skin damage and the development of skin cancer...

We all coat our skins dutifully with sunscreen and smugly think it's a job well done. However, just when you thought it was safe, a new danger rears its ugly head. An article published in the *British Medical Journal* has claimed that sunscreens containing oxybenzone (usually those with a higher sun protection factor or SPF – yes, the ones we merrily soak our small children with, to keep them safe) give users a higher risk of developing malignant skin cancer. Oxybenzone is used to filter ultraviolet light, converting it from light to heat on the surface of the skin. So far so good – so you would think. Unfortunately, the *BMJ* report tells us that the light may well be converted to heat in the basal layers of the skin – and this means that damage to growing cells is likely.

As early as 1998, US scientists found that sunscreens protect us from sunburn and carcinomas, but they do not protect us against melanoma. Melanomas have increased twenty-fold in Europe and the US since 1935. We probably aren't spending more time outside than our ancestors – many of whom may have worked outside – but there were a couple of decades when people thought a tan was healthy and regularly basted themselves for a beach or pool-side frying session. However, it is worth considering that in protecting ourselves from carcinomas, we may well have declared open season for melanomas by using certain types of sunscreen. We put on protective creams and lotions, and think we can stay out longer in the sun. It seems that this may well not be the case.

Para-amino-benzoic acid (PABA) is another common ingredient in sunscreen. It works like oxybenzone, absorbing UV rays. An Oxford University scientist, John Knowland, has found that PABA damages DNA and thus increases the risk of skin cancer. Another sun filter, butyl methoxydibenzoylmethane (which filters UVA) has been

Here's an idea for you...

As it is believed that beta carotene can help to protect the skin against sun damage, add some to your diet. The body converts beta carotene into vitamin A as it needs it. Look for yellow, orange and red vegetables and fruits such as carrots, peppers, sweet potatoes, pumpkin, mango and ruby grapefruit. Also add dark green and leafy vegetables such as watercress, kale, broccoli, brussels sprouts, spinach, parsley, asparagus, courgettes and peas. Try to eat the vegetables fresh in salads and stir fries to get the greatest benefit from them. Alternatively, make some soup: carrot and pumpkin, red pepper, tomato and fresh parley, sweet potato and yellow pepper – design your own beta-carotene-rich delight.

89

found to be unstable in sunlight (!). This means it can break down into chemicals that inhibit the skin's natural defence against damage leaving it vulnerable to premature ageing and cancer.

Other common ingredients may cause skin irritation. Cinnimates, for example, have been found to have hormone-disrupting effects. Chemicals that mimic oestrogen, if applied regularly, can lead to breast and ovarian cancers in women and may cause gender-bending effects in men.

Natural alternatives
There are some healthier alternatives around, such as the range of sunscreens combining organic skin creams with sun protection factors (SPF) up to factor 15 that the company Green People has created. They use natural antioxidants extracted from organic green tea, edelweiss, olive leaf and rosemary, which have natural UV filters. They also contain echinacea, myrrh and aloe vera for their soothing/healing properties. Tin oxide may also be used to completely block the rays of the sun and calamine lotion (based on zinc oxide) is also useful as a sun blocker. It is thought that these substances are much safer than PABA or oxybenzone-based sunscreens.

Diet may also have a part to play in protecting the skin from the effects of the sun's rays. Recent evidence suggests that a low-fat diet supplemented with particular vitamins and antioxidants can help. A diet that neutralises free radicals (which can cause DNA mutations) can help to counteract the damaging effects of solar radiation. A balanced, wholefood diet containing lots of antioxidant vitamins and minerals such as beta carotene, vitamins C and E and the minerals selenium, zinc, copper and manganese help to neutralise free radicals.

Good skin begins with just taking care of it.

Ian Ginsberg, pharmacist and businessman

How did it go?

Q. With all the news about the damage the sun's rays can do to our skins, should we avoid it completely?

A. In moderation, the sun can be beneficial. It helps the body to make vitamin D, for example. But be careful to plan any sun-drenched outdoor activities to avoid the sun's strongest rays, between around 11 a.m. and 3 p.m. Wear loose cotton clothes and a hat to minimise exposure, and wear sunglasses that provide 100% UV ray protection. In short, enjoy the sunshine – but remember to be cautious.

Q. I keep reading about how important it is to watch moles. It's all a bit confusing. What am I supposed to look out for, though?

A. The American Cancer Society has a useful list of A B C D warning signs to look out for; they should help. A is for Asymmetry: watch out for any changes in the shape of the mole. B is Border: look for any irregularity or changes in the edges of the mole. Have the borders blurred at all? Is it harder to see where the mole ends and ordinary skin begins? C is Colour: has the colour of the mole changed at all? Are there irregular shades of brown, blue, or black visible? Has pigmentation been lost in all or a portion of the mole? Finally, D – Diameter: has the mole increased in size? If any mole has a diameter greater than six millimetres, have it looked at by your medical practitioner straight away.

21. Vegetable vitality

Grow your own vegetables – in containers, raised beds or a vegetable plot – and you'll taste the difference!

Some things will work well for you; others less so; it's all a case of trial and error.

We grow as many vegetables on our organic smallholding as we can, and grow them in a variety of ways. Some are in rows in conventional beds and others are grown in mixed beds with ornamentals – many vegetables (such as ruby chard with their glowing stems) will give the most beautiful flowers a run for their money. We also grow in containers. Organic vegetables taste better, have the health benefits associated with a lack of pesticides, and growing your own is cheap. Whatever the size of your plot – even if you have no garden at all – there are organic vegetables you can grow.

In containers

You can grow many vegetables in containers. Small, tender ones such as baby carrots, cut-and-come-again salads, radishes and new potatoes are easy to grow in pots and half-barrels. Peas, runner beans and green beans can all be grown in pots with a firmly anchored support, and even greedy feeders such as courgettes, pumpkins and squash can be grown in large containers. The key is to make sure you have well-nourished soil with good drainage. Drainage is easy to arrange – broken pieces of polystyrene packaging are light and a layer will do the job well. Alternatively, pea gravel or the old standby of broken pieces of terracotta pot are also fine. Make sure your soil is well fed to ensure maximum growth. Add lots of your own nutritious compost if possible; alternatively add organic feed. This can be a certified organic feed, like Growganic seaweed extract, or it can be a home-made version created by chopping comfrey and stuffing it into the foot of a pair of tights before soaking it in water for a couple of weeks. You'll want to do this outside though, because it stinks! To use, add some of the dark brown liquid to a full watering can (one part to ten of water). Finally, make sure you are careful about watering. Allow the surface of the soil to feel dry to the touch; overwatering is more dangerous than underwatering as plant roots rot.

In the garden

Think creatively about planting schemes. You don't have to plant veggies in regimented lines (although I confess a certain satisfaction with the small area I have planted in this way – it reminds me of my parents' allotment). You can integrate vegetables into your garden easily. Think of your garden in layers, and that will help. Tripods of beans give your garden height, and provide amazing quantities of food. Heritage varieties in particular have large, fragrant flowers and are very ornamental. In the UK, Garden Organic organise the Heritage Seed Library (HSL). This is a collection of seeds no longer available commercially and is well worth every penny of the membership fees.

Here's an idea for you...

Making a raised bed is really easy. I've built mine with bark-coated slabwood, but anything will do as long as it is not treated with preservatives or other chemicals – no second-hand railway sleepers. Measure out your bed and knock in a 60 cm wooden peg cut from at least 5 cm x 5 cm wood at each corner. Nail your wood to the pegs to make the bed. Top it up with organic compost and start planting!

Next add colourful, lower-growing plants such as rainbow chard, variegated herbs such as sage and scrambling plants – squash and small pumpkins. These will grow happily alongside ornamentals and the system encourages the beneficial insects that become a part of organic growing. Growing a variety of plants reduces the likelihood of pests and diseases. It also looks beautiful and will give you an immense amount of pleasure as you watch the vegetables grow and swell.

You might want to build yourself a raised bed for your veggies. They are easy to maintain, and the higher the sides of the bed the easier. Drainage is good in raised beds and they're a great option for a house on a new housing estate with less than perfect soil in its new, rubble-filled garden. Raised beds can be planted more densely which leaves less room for invading weeds, and give you a longer growing season as effective drainage means the soil warms more quickly in the spring. You can also add a cold frame (or a plastic sheeting cover) to the top of your bed to warm the soil before planting and to hold off the first frosts.

Nothing is better than freshly grown food, straight from the garden, with no added chemicals. It's the ultimate taste experience!

The act of putting into your mouth what the earth has grown is perhaps your most direct interaction with the earth.

Frances Moore Lappé, *Diet For A Small Planet*, 1971

How did it go?

Q. I've seen a lot about heritage vegetables in magazines – purple carrots and the like. Isn't this all a bit of a fad like decking?

A. They're actually more than a fashion statement, though they do look attractive. Many traditional varieties are disappearing as most commercial seed company catalogues are dominated by modern FI hybrids. These specially bred seeds give higher yields than the old varieties, but tend to be less hardy and disease resistant. Seeds saved from them don't usually breed true, unlike traditional ones, so growers have to buy new seed annually. Growing heritage varieties increases biodiversity and is a small step towards conserving varieties that would otherwise die out.

Q. I don't have acres of space, so I don't want to grow in rows. I've heard about forest gardening, but would that be any good for a suburban garden?

A. It can work well, even in small plots, as it maximises the use of the ground while working in harmony with nature. In a forest garden, plants are grown together in a way similar to natural woodland – in layers. Trees and shrubs produce edible crops such as fruit and nuts, and perennial herbs and vegetables grow underneath. Such a garden can still produce a good crop even if you spend little time on it. Look for a course to make sure you understand the principles; try your local agricultural college.

22. The natural nursery

When you have a baby, you want only the best for your child – and the organic baby gets the best.

Are all the media stories about our toxic world just scaremongering, or are there things that, as a parent, you really need to avoid?

When you have a baby, you're bombarded with information and decisions need to be made about everything from feeding to where the little mite is going to sleep. Unfortunately, you also become hypersensitive to news about all of the latest hidden dangers and toxins lurking – well, to everything, actually. Let's look at some basics.

Bath and skin products

Your skin is your body's largest organ, and it is affected by whatever it comes in contact with. Skin is thirsty, and absorbs substances into your body. Think about it: some medicines are taken via skin patches. The substances you put on your skin end up, to some degree, inside your body.

A recent study published in the *Journal of Paediatrics* claimed that using baby bath products increases the amount of phthalates in babies' urine. Phthalates have been shown to affect reproductive development (there's even a suggestion that they can cause early-onset puberty) and to have a causal link to the development of allergies and eczema. Phthalates are used to stabilise fragrances and make plastics flexible. Most baby bath products also contain SLS (sodium laureth sulphate) which is the ingredient that makes bubble bath, well, bubbly. It also unfortunately irritates the skin, causing eczema and dermatitis. A definite no-no for sensitive baby skin!

Parabens are chemicals added to soaps and shampoos to act as a preservative. Research has shown that parabens are potentially carcinogenic and act as xenoestrogens (an oestrogen increaser).That's bad enough in products used by adults; worse still in babies who absorb almost three times the chemicals in soaps and bath products that adults do.

Another ingredient to avoid is DEA (diethanolamine). DEA is found in baby bubble baths, soaps, lotions and shampoos. It has been linked with kidney, liver and other organ damage, and is another potential carcinogen. As with many other chemicals, research has found that DEA has cumulative toxicity, as it cannot be excreted. It builds up in the fatty tissues with repeated skin exposure.

So, where can you find products to protect your little treasures? Luckily there are many manufacturers to choose from. Pur sell a lovely organic range including chamomile baby wash, lavender and mandarin baby oil (great for massage too), organic nipple balm for mum (important for her skin safety and because it goes in junior's mouth) and organic stretch-mark butter. Free Spirit Organics sell delightful 'faerie bubbles' bath (my nine year old still loves this!), so explore cyberspace and see what you fancy.

Here's an idea for you...

Instead of a teething ring, give your baby edibles to chomp away at. Bagels and toast sticks are great as they don't break apart too easily and are easy for a young child to hold. Vegetables such as carrots and cucumbers are great soothers because they can be chilled in the fridge beforehand to help cool inflamed gums. Also give your baby a veggie stick large enough not to be swallowed, but small enough to hold. Be cautious: never let your baby chew on anything without supervision and remember to wash all vegetables (including organic ones) before you give them to your baby.

Toys

Baby toys are often made from brightly coloured synthetic materials, many containing phthalates (especially PVC toys) – and teething babies chew on them for hours. Constantly wet, constantly in the mouth, these toys can leach chemicals that are then ingested by your baby. There is a Europe-wide ruling which bans phthalates in baby toys 'intended to be put into the mouths of children under three' – which covers things like teething rings – but this law doesn't cover other baby toys. If you have a baby, you'll know that everything goes in the mouth, so make sure the toys you choose are safe by opting for natural materials such as organic cotton, wool, etc. Do some online research, and check out Sckoon, who make a good range including a very cute organic bunny.

Bedding

Moses baskets and cribs are useful for daytime naps, and some people (not me) like cots. If you have a baby bed, you need a baby mattress. Little Green Earthlets sell a good range of organic mattresses so babies don't breathe in chemicals as they sleep. The coco mat filled with organic coir (coconut husks) and wrapped in lambswool is rather lovely; it is treated with lavender, lemon and eucalyptus extracts to guard against dust mites. Again, examine your options carefully before you buy.

When you are a mother, you are never alone in your thoughts. A mother always has to think twice, once for herself and once for her child.

Sophia Loren

How did it go?

Q. I can see the point in making organic baby food as it goes in their bodies, but is it really worth shelling out for organic baby clothes?

A. A baby's skin is five times thinner than that of an adult, so it is easier for toxins to enter through it. Cotton is the most heavily sprayed crop in the world, and cotton – in various forms – is a popular fabric for baby wear. Organic baby garments are free from pesticide residue. There are many options, and you could even have a go at making some organic cotton, wool or hemp clothes yourself. Even if they are a slightly funny shape, you'll get immense satisfaction from the exercise, save money – and babies don't care as long as they're snuggly.

Q. I'm a bit worried about baby oil; it smells great but it's a petroleum derivative. Should I buy an organic variety?

A. Mineral oil – standard baby oil – can irritate skin and block pores as it lies on the surface of the skin, trapping moisture; it's not absorbed. Try a natural organic oil instead; my favourite is sweet almond oil, but you can use any light oil. Olive oil is a great treatment for any dry patches your baby develops and can be used to treat cradle cap. Incidentally, don't use baby talc as inhalation can be dangerous; go for organic corn starch. Totally safe; feels silky on the skin.

23. Love your laundry!

Love it or hate it, we all have laundry. But do we really need the baffling array of cleaning products that stare back at us from the supermarket shelves?

How can you make sure your clothes get cleaned properly without polluting the environment in the process?

It's one of the weekly chores – sort the washing, load the washing, pour gallons of chemicals on the washing… but do you need to? The short answer is no. Think about it – most of the clothes you wash (unless you're a mud wrestler – and then you probably don't wear too many clothes) aren't that dirty, despite what the ads say otherwise.

The bulk of the clothes which get washed regularly are probably just sweaty, unless you are a parent to a small child and then you have my heartfelt sympathy. Sweat does not take industrial-strength detergent to shift it; powerfully swooshing hot water, courtesy of your washing machine, will take care of it. So perhaps we should all think twice before adding washing powder, typically containing a cocktail of phosphates, formaldehyde, enzymes, sodium lauryl sulphate (a foaming agent that makes the water sudsy), pesticide residues, chlorine bleach (chlorine reacts with organic materials in the environment to create potentially carcinogenic compounds such as chloroform and certain organophosphates which cause reproductive and immune system disorders), titanium oxide – and that's without all the synthetic fragrances and colours! There have been suggestions that the artificial musks found in washing powder can cause liver damage. Harsh laundry products can cause terrible allergic reactions in susceptible people – especially children.

Many of these chemicals also have an impact on the environment. Phosphates enter water courses, polluting rivers and lakes and killing wildlife. Petroleum-based chemicals in powders and washing liquids do not completely degrade, so the pollutants build up over time, damaging the environment.

Alternatives

Ecologically sound washing products are already available. Ecover make a range of washing liquids, powders, cleaning products and dishwasher salts, and many local health food shops and major supermarkets stock them in the UK. Sonett also manufacture a range of organic washing products, including washing liquid. It is free from synthetic preservatives, fragrances or dyes, enzymes and petroleum-based ingredients. This detergent is great in areas of water hardness and can be used at low temperatures – saving precious energy. The product is derived from rape seed oil, sugar surfactants, fatty alcohol sulphate and organic lavender essential oil.

Soapnuts are a brilliant, completely natural product. The soap nut tree (*Spanidus mukorossi*) produces fruit in nut shells. The shells release saponin which creates soapy suds when it comes into contact with warm water. You put around six

Here's an idea for you...

You can also naturally bleach clothes with organic lemon juice and sunshine. It makes you feel good just thinking about it! Just add half a cup of lemon juice to the rinse cycle of your machine or, even better, make up a bucket of water and lemon juice and leave your whites to soak. Hang your clothes outside on the line to dry. You don't need to wander backwards and forwards sniffing deeply as the clothes billow in the breeze – but it's a wonderful experience… as the ad says, 'Mmmm, lemony'.

103

shells in a little cotton bag and add it to the washing machine. Eco balls are also excellent. The system uses three balls with foam rings that work by ionising the water, lifting the dirt out of your clothes. Apart from being good for the environment, Eco balls are hypoallergenic and so are great for people with sensitive skin. Dryer balls are also a useful addition to the organic laundry. You add them to the tumble dryer, and they reduce drying time by 25%. They soften clothes naturally, by moving about in the tumble dryer, which makes any type of fabric softener redundant. They also reduce lint and static. Of course, you could always just hang the washing out on the line…

Try some homespun laundry products, too. You can use things you make yourself to clean the house – and that includes the laundry. For example, make your own fabric conditioner. Mix together two cups of white wine vinegar (a general purpose super-household-cleaner if ever I saw one!), two cups of baking soda, and four cups of water. Combine these slowly over a sink because they will fizz like an Ibizan foam party. Keep the mix in a plastic bottle and add a quarter of a cup to your final rinse cycle. The vinegar will remove all soap scum and the mixture will soften your fabrics; the vinegar smell disperses once the garments have dried.

We should all do what, in the long run, gives us joy, even if it is only picking grapes or sorting the laundry.

E. B. White, US writer

How did it go?

Q. Why aren't scientists developing safer laundry products?

A. Some researchers are actually trying. Scientists at the University of Bath, for example, are researching to find a new chemical made from plant oils and sugar. This detergent would make washing powder and bathing products less damaging to the environment. It is in the interests of large manufacturers to support this type of research as the 'green economy' is booming, and consumers are driving developments as they become more aware of the dangers of conventional chemicals.

Q. I like using those bottles of perfumed water in my steam iron to make the sheets smell nice. I've heard a lot of them contain nasty chemicals though. Any ideas for alternatives?

A. You can make wonderful natural ironing water with distilled water (better for your iron) and essential oils. Traditionally, lavender water has been used to freshen laundry, but just choose your favourite organic essential oil. I like ylang-ylang and neroli for the bedsheets – very sensual. Add a small quantity of essential oil (only about an eighth of a teaspoon) to a litre of water. Always shake well before every use to disperse the oil. If you have a steam iron with a water compartment, add the scented water there. If you have a non-steam iron, put your water in an empty spray bottle and mist your laundry as you iron.

24. Bin the bleach – natural hair colouring and care

We all want lovely locks, and many of us – men included – use all manner of dyes, potions and lotions to make it happen...

But despite their claims of natural ingredients and botanical additions, how safe are they?

Shampoo and conditioners

Healthy hair is shiny and full of body. We've all seen the commercials of models with beautiful, flowing hair. But that lustre and bounce may come with health costs attached as lots of nasties lurk in those pretty bottles. For example, the detergent sodium lauryl sulphate (SLS) is found in 90% of commercial shampoos and conditioners as well as in bath and shower gels, bubble bath and cleansers. SLS is also found in car washing liquid, engine de-greaser and garage floor cleaner, as it powerfully cleans greasy surfaces. Still keen to use those floral shampoos? There's more. SLS clears away grease – but it does so corrosively. This means it strips natural fats and lipids from skin and hair, so they cannot regulate their own natural moisture levels. Skin may become inflamed and infected, and hair loss may occur as the follicle is damaged. Exposure to SLS can also affect breathing, causing laryngitis and shortness of breath. Nausea, vomiting and headaches have also been attributed to SLS exposure, according to the Material Safety Data Sheet produced by the US government. Heard enough yet? There's even more bad news.

A study carried out by the University of Georgia Medical College found that SLS penetrates the eyes, brain, liver and heart. It is retained long term in the organs, and can cause cell membranes to degenerate, which can damage your immune system. SLS can cause blindness, as the protein in the eye is prevented from forming properly. This can lead to cataracts, especially when SLS penetrates the eyes of young children.

SLS has also been found to react with many of the other ingredients used in cosmetics to create nitrates, which are possibly carcinogenic. The nature of SLS – the way it has the ability to penetrate the skin and be absorbed – means that any chemicals present are absorbed easily by your body. There are loads of organic alternatives out there.

Hair colours and bleaches

It's fun to change the colour of your hair, but as a long-time user of the bleach bottle I was horrified to find the wide variety of damaging ingredients found in hair colourants. Most contain ammonia and/or bleach. This is bad news for your hair, as it strips it of oils and proteins, and weakens the shaft. Health-wise, it is also bad news. Most darker hair colourings contain paraphenylenediamine (PPD). This chemical can cause allergic reactions including dermatitis and eye problems. It can also make you

Here's an idea for you...

If you want to lighten your hair, try rhubarb. No joke – it's an old family secret. Chop five or six rhubarb stalks into a pan of water (500 ml) and leave to simmer until the rhubarb turns to mush. Sieve the liquid and chuck the rhubarb mush onto the compost heap. Add a cup of chamomile flowers (available from most health-food shops or online) and simmer for twenty minutes. Your kitchen will smell like summer! Strain, and comb the liquid through dry hair. Sit in the sun – it helps the process. Leave for an hour, then rinse. And to ensure your locks are in tip-top condition, comb organic sweet almond oil through your hair and leave that for an hour.

susceptible to cross-sensitisation, which means you become allergic to many other substances similar to PPD, such as textile dyes, ink, petrol, food dyes and many preservatives. This can make life in the modern world rather difficult, unless your idea of fun includes wearing a medic-alert bracelet and carrying an Epi-Pen at all times.

There are increasing numbers of natural hair colourants on the market as a response to consumer concerns. Logona produce a range that are free from parabens, phthalates, synthetic fragrances, petroleum or mineral based oils, preservatives, ammonia, peroxide or any chemical colourings. Be aware that natural hair colourants do not usually give as strong coverage as chemical types, and they cannot lighten your shade substantially. You may need several applications to achieve the desired shade, and exact resulting shades are hard to predict. On the plus side, they coat your hair cuticle, making it smooth and glossy. This adds condition and a beautiful sheen.

Finally, be wary of brands that market themselves as natural products but are anything but. Always read the labels to check ingredients. I have been caught a few times in health-food stores looking at lovely green boxes with botanical prints on – only to find the product still contains PPD.

I'm not offended by all the dumb-blonde jokes because I know that I'm not dumb. I also know I'm not blonde.

Dolly Parton

How did it go?

Q. I have coloured my hair for years and would like to change to using a natural colourant. I know some hair-colour products say 'not suitable for use with previously dyed hair' – is that the case with natural products?

A. Remember the mantra: always carry out a strand test. It is not likely, but it is possible that using herbal colours straight after chemical hair colours will result in some discolouration or odd results. If you think you may still have traces of a chemical dye left in your hair, a strand test will help you to determine the result. Take two small strands from different parts of your head – at the nape of your neck is naturally darkest, and your brow tends to be lightest because of the sun's effects. Apply the colourant to both strands, leave for the recommended time and rinse. Dry before examining the results.

Q. How come hair products are available containing dangerous chemicals? Is anything being done to make hair colourant safer?

A. We have a choice; we do not have to dye our hair. However, in December 2006, the European Commission introduced a ban on twenty-two chemicals used in hair dyes, following a study linking long-term use to a risk of bladder cancer. Moves are obviously being made to make things safer, but in the meantime natural alternatives may be the best way forward. Knowledge of the dangers has made me change the habits of a lifetime.

25. Mermaid magic

If you're worried about the chemicals in the bath products you buy, why not harvest some herbs, find some flowers – and make your own?

Try some of the recipes below and you'll soon be a bathing beauty.

With all the worry about sodium laureth sulphate (SLS) and parabens in cosmetic preparations, many people are looking for alternatives. When you have a bath every day, it can be expensive to keep buying organic bath preparations, wonderful though many are. Making your own is easy; you'll soon wonder why you didn't try it before!

Herb bath

This is incredibly simple. Collect a handful of the herbs you like best, and tie them into a rough cotton or muslin fabric bag. I make my own, but you can buy them from many herbal supply shops. The bag is tied under the running tap so the herbs infuse into the water, like a giant teabag. When I first took herbal baths, I just chucked the herbs into the water. It looked and smelled great but I was picking bits out of my hair for days, and the bath was a beast to clean.

Lavender is easy to grow and makes for a stimulating bath, as does mint. Lemon verbena, mixed with a few chunks of organic lemon rind, makes a zingy, fresh fragrance. Violets make a relaxing, sensuous bath – but experiment, and find your own favourites.

Bath salts

I actually use sea salt for a mineral rich bath that's great for aching muscles. Fill a jar in layers with sea salt crystals, interspersed with your chosen herb. I find sprigs of rosemary work well. Leave the salt in a warm place such as the airing cupboard for a couple of weeks so the salt becomes infused with the herb. Drop a handful into a hot bath and wait for it to dissolve (unless you want to exfoliate your bum rather radically).

Bath milk

A milk bath sounds weird – but if it was good enough for Cleopatra, it's good enough for us! Combine a couple of cups of organic powdered milk with two tablespoons of dried rose petals (home grown or bought from an organic supplier), two tablespoons of lavender flowers, and six to eight drops of essential oil (I like neroli or patchouli – that could, of course, be because I'm an old hippie,

Here's an idea for you...

Tone and buff your skin with a body scrub. Add enough olive oil to a cup of sea salt to make a paste, then add a few drops of your favourite scented oil or a few drops of tea-tree oil if you have any blemishes. Play about and blend your favourites – ylang-ylang and neroli make a gorgeous blend. Scrub dry skin with the mix and then shower off, and it will leave your skin beautifully soft. Oatmeal also makes a good scrub, gentle enough for delicate skin.

so experiment until you find your own favourite). Keep the powdered milk bath in a glass jar by the bath and add it to your cotton bag, then suspend it under running water. It makes your skin incredibly soft!

Bath oils

Use an organic base oil such as olive for dry skin, or almond for normal skin. I prefer almond oil as it is much lighter and disperses better in the hot water. Add sprigs of your favourite herbs to the oil and leave it on a sunny windowsill. I leave mine for a couple of weeks, fishing out the old sprig of herbs and adding fresh ones after a week for maximum strength. Again, rosemary or lavender works well but try different types to find your favourite.

Bath bombs

These are just great fun – to make, and to use. Just be careful if you have sensitive skin as the ingredients can be drying. My daughters and I have gone so far as to buy specially shaped moulds (easily obtainable via online suppliers and ebay) to make our bombs in the shape of stars or goddesses – if you're going to do it, sometimes it's fun to go the whole hog! You need citric acid, corn starch, sodium bicarbonate, the essential oils of your choice, almond oil and any herbs or flowers you wish to include.

Mix the dry ingredients in a bowl. I use four parts sodium bicarbonate to one part citric acid and one part corn starch. In a small container, mix the almond oil and a few drops of essential oil. Slowly drizzle the oil onto the dry ingredients, mixing as you go. As soon as the mixture sticks together when you press it, you have added enough. Either push the mixture into moulds or make small balls. Leave the bath bombs to dry for one to two days before storing them – obviously in a dry container unless you want to look like a mad professor, mid experiment! Add to the bath as required.

An oil massage, a hot bath, a good night's sleep, soft smells and music and clothes with soft textures denote sensuality to me.

Padma Lakshmi, actress and author

How did it go?

Q. Can I use baby oil to make bath preparations? I have seen large bottles selling really cheaply.

A. Apart from the fact that baby oil is usually a petroleum derivative, and therefore not perhaps the healthiest oil to use in bath preparations, it is not suitable because it rests on the surface of the skin, making it greasy. Instead, use olive oil, avocado oil or one of the lighter oils such as almond. These penetrate the skin and keep it smooth and supple.

Q. I'd like to make some organic face packs. Any ideas?

A. That's an easy one. For a face mask that smells delicious and leaves your skin brighter, liquidise a few slices of cucumber and spread them on your face. Mashed banana is a truly lickable mask and natural yoghurt is soothing. Organic fullers' earth is a clay material to which you can add a few drops of essential oil. Mix it with a little water and spread the paste on your face. As it dries out you will feel your skin tighten; the clay draws excess oil and impurities out.

26. Pretty pure – organic skin care

The things that you put on your skin enter your bloodstream – so keep the nasty chemicals out, and pamper yourself with some organic skincare products.

If you've ever read the ingredients on your favourite moisturiser, you may have wondered what you're slapping on your face...

For a woman in her forties, my skin doesn't look too shabby. That could be genetics; it also has to do with the fact that I have never smoked and I'd like to think I look after my skin. Now, in moments of weakness over the years I have been seduced by all manner of expensive goodies full of pseudo-scientific this and that, but they haven't really delivered. Combine that with worries about the safety of products (don't forget that skin is the body's biggest organ and it absorbs the things we rub into it), the natural way just might be the answer.

In recent years, partly due to downshifting and growing my own, I have experimented with lots of home-made products. But when it comes to skincare, I have been trying out some wonderful organic ones. This is because I can slather them on, safe in the knowledge that they don't contain commonly used ingredients such as butylated hydroxytoluene (a preservative which has been linked with cancers), parabens (linked with cancers; can disrupt the hormones as they mimic oestrogen), and sodium lauryl sulphate (possibly carcinogenic) among other harsh chemical nasties such as fragrances and colours that can cause allergic reactions.

As with anything, you need to experiment to find what works best for you. There are a huge range of organic skin creams on the market, so give them a try (many suppliers sell sample sizes so you can test drive before committing yourself). Here are some suggestions.

For ageing skin

Hmm. That would be me. I need a cream that can deal with dry patches, smooth wrinkles and cope with the odd breakout without feeling greasy or heavy on my skin. Just a miracle needed there, then. I look for products that contain GLA (gamma-linolenic acid). This may be found in evening primrose oil, or at even higher concentrations, in borage oil. Rosehip seed oil is also a magic bullet for ageing skin as it is rich in omega-3 fatty acids, which are powerful antioxidants. Great creams to try for this type of skin include Crème de la Crème (containing borage and rosehip seed oil) from Free Spirit Organics, Trilogy Energising Face Lotion with Rosehip Oil (containing rosehip and evening primrose oils, extracts of green tea, ginkgo biloba and vitamin E) from Rose Pure, and the Australian

Here's an idea for you...

Surf the Internet to find suppliers of organic skincare ranges. Many suppliers offer sample sachets free of charge so you can try before you buy. Others offer free samples of a variety of products with a minimum purchase, and many offer small sample pots so you can try a product without splashing out on a full-size pot. Check out what's available, and ask if nothing is offered. Thy can only say no…

product Rejuvenessence Facial Serum (containing rosehip oil, jojoba oil, avocado oil and safflower oil) from Miessence. Most organic cosmetic ranges carry products for ageing skin, so sample a few and find what works best with yours.

Teenage skin

Teenagers are often plagued with spots and blackheads – a horrible but usually passing phase. Don't be tempted to use harsh chemicals on the skin; they can leave people feeling sore and just exacerbate the problem, leaving skin flaky and red. Use products that contain mild astringents, such as witch hazel to lift oil, and antibacterials such as tea-tree oil. Soothing ingredients, such as wheatgerm oil, will help to reduce redness and inflammation. Good products to try include Living Facial Cleanser (containing witch hazel and tea tree) from Raw Gaia, Nutritone lotion (containing soothing aloe vera and tea tree) from Rio Trading, or Thera Neem soap (containing 25% neem oil, an antibacterial, antiviral, antifungal, anti-inflammatory) from Organix. When choosing products for teenagers, remember to go for gentle formulations which will soothe rather than inflame problem skin. Remind them never to pick at their skin or squeeze spots – however tempting – as it will spread infection and may even lead to scarring. If your teen has severe problems it may be worth consulting a homeopath for extra help from the inside out.

Beauty is only skin deep, but it's a valuable asset if you're poor or haven't any sense.

Vernon Howard, author

How did it go?

Q. My husband has seen the effects of the organic creams and lotions I use, and would like to use organic skincare products such as shaving cream and aftershave. Are there any ranges especially made for men?

A. Well, skin is skin – and organic healthy skincare ranges are made with all skin in mind, whether it's butch manskin or something more girly! If he feels a bit threatened by any botanical pictures on bottles (ahem!), or if he's looking for shaving cream, etc., get him to look at the brilliantly named Herban Cowboy range. Lavera carry a wide range of organic products aimed specifically at men, and he might also like Florame Aromatherapy's shaving foam which contains cedar and lavender oil as well as peppermint leaf water.

Q. I am a vegetarian, so prefer to use cosmetics and creams without the use of animal by-products. How can I be sure that the creams I use are suitable for my lifestyle choices?

A. Most organic skincare products (but not all) are made using vegetable-only sources of materials such as glycerine (note that if a product lists glycerine, rather than vegetable glycerine, on the pack it is likely to be of animal origin and is a slaughterhouse by-product). To be absolutely sure, contact suppliers; a simple email to the company will get you the information you need. You can also consult the UK's Vegetarian Society; they run yearly awards for vegetarian, cruelty-free body and skincare ranges, so they are a great source of useful information. Check out BUAV's *Little Book of Cruelty Free*, available on their website, too.

27. Mother Earth

We want the best for our babies and toddlers. As food scares about BSE, GM foods and pesticide usage increasingly make the news, many people are turning to organic baby food.

The best way to be sure that what your child is eating is actually safe is to make your own baby food.

In December 2000, the Pesticide Residues Committee (PRC) revealed in a report that pesticide residues which may disrupt the hormone system had been found in baby food. Carbendazim was found in baby food made by Heinz and Milupa; it affects the production of sperm and damages testicular development. The contaminated brands were not organic. In recent years, many baby food producers have moved to completely organic production; other large brands now have organic ranges. But there have been other safety scares. In 2003, the European Food Safety Authority reported that the chemical semicarbizide had been found in baby food. This chemical can damage DNA, and has been linked to cancers, liver damage and birth abnormalities. Worryingly, the toxin was traced to the plastic gaskets used to seal glass baby food jars – which meant no brands using this technology were free from chemicals. The UK's Food Standards Agency (FSA) controversially advised parents to 'play it safe' and make their own baby food (but did not go so far as to advise against buying jars of commercially produced food). Food manufacturers were instructed to find new methods of sealing jars to safeguard against contamination.

For busy parents, this is all worrying news. You want the best for your baby (and having a baby suddenly makes you look really closely at the safety of everything), but ready-made food, with its portability and convenience, is just so attractive. So what are your options?

Ready-made organic baby food

Many brands are now available, with Organix being one of the most popular in the UK. They provide a wide range of foods from puree for babies just starting on solids, to finger food for toddlers and wholegrain healthy food for older children. Hipp are a long-established company providing ready made baby and toddler food, and Plum Organics make an interesting range of frozen foods. Type 'organic baby foods' into your search engine and you will get a flavour (sadly, pun intended) of the huge range available. Organic baby food is big business and a limited range is likely to be available in most supermarkets.

Home-made baby food

Making organic baby food is very easy. I've made baby food for each of my children, using the odd carton of baby cereal as back up. For the youngest babies, just beginning with solids, fruit and vegetable purees are the easiest thing in the world. Cook the vegetables, zapp them in the blender – and that's it. Never be tempted to add seasonings; at best they are unnecessary and, at worst (like salt), positively dangerous. Think about it – it's weird enough tasting seasoning-free

Here's an idea for you...

Make your own breakfast cereal. This recipe is suitable for children from around seven months, when babies are eating lumpier textures. It's great for toddlers, older children (and you!) too. Mix porridge oats, a chopped apple and sultanas in a pan. Add enough apple juice to cover the dry ingredients and bring to the boil. Simmer for about ten minutes until the sultanas are plump and juicy. Remove from the heat and chop a banana into the mixture. When it's cool enough, serve. It's lovely on cold winter mornings, with added cinnamon for parents.

sweet potato or even carrot for the first time ever, as your baby's 'I've possibly eaten the most amazing thing in the universe' comedy face will attest. I used to make batches of baby glop and freeze it in ice-cube trays for defrosting as only tiny portions are needed at first. These days you can buy all manner of special freezer containers and tiny electric grinders especially for making baby food, but these seem like a bit of a faff. The old 'make a batch and freeze it for convenience' routine was popular for a reason. It worked.

Finger foods for older babies and toddlers are easy. Fingers of raw veggies are great for teething (chill them in the fridge) with a bit of nutrition thrown in. Talking of throwing, your carpets are now fair game for all manner of goo and slop, expertly directed by your baby. Invest in a plastic mat for under the table at feeding time, or consider installing wood or ceramic floors as part of your late pregnancy nesting frenzy. Even if you are knackered, wipe up food spills immediately after feeding time at the zoo finishes. I'd like to say I'm suggesting that purely for hygiene, but I was remembering with horror the way baby slop dries to a cement-like texture that is nigh on impossible to remove from most surfaces. You have been warned.

There is nothing better for your baby than making your own fresh baby food, and it is cheaper than buying the commercial variety.

Annabel Karmel, baby food guru, re-emphasising the point!

How did it go?

Q. *Is it OK to serve mushed up versions of our family meals to our toddler?*

A. Your toddler will enjoy eating family meals, and being just like mum and dad. Eating at the table with the rest of the family makes your toddler understand that meal times are for food, but are also about togetherness and shared news. It is a good idea to get them used to the type of food you cook. Just remember not to add salt or salty food to the meal (also good for you, as well as vital for your toddler's immature kidneys which cannot process salt efficiently), and offer your child rice meals, pasta and other family food.

Q. *How can I teach my toddler about healthy eating without making it an issue?*

A. Safely involve your child in cooking your meals whenever possible, whether it's making pastry together or shelling peas. Talk about the food as you make it and your toddler will learn about healthy eating and cooking almost by osmosis.

28. Blissful bedrooms

There's nothing nicer than a light airy bedroom and crisp, clean sheets to give you a good night's sleep – so why not go the whole hog and make bedtime an organic experience?

How to make your bedroom into an oasis of calm.

Your bedroom is the room where you spend one-third of your life. It should be the place where you restore yourself for the rigours of life in the real world. So your bedroom should be as healthy as it can be – and that means making it free from allergens and using organic materials wherever possible. Modern bedding is often made from synthetic fabric, which often contains petrochemicals or their by-products. Even if it is made from cotton, the crops may have been grown using large amounts of pesticides. A conventionally grown cotton T-shirt can have as many as seventeen full teaspoons of pesticide residue in the finished product – so think how much a set of cotton bedding and a cotton-coated mattress could contain! Research shows that we absorb chemicals into our bodies from our environment, so we need to be cautious.

To reduce indoor air pollution in the form of pollen, VOCs (volatile organic chemicals) and dust mites, keep your bedroom well ventilated. Open a window when you get up in the morning, and make sure you air your mattress on a weekly basis. I prop my mattress up when I change the bed so the air can circulate. Likewise, don't be too quick to make your bed. The bedding could do with an airing when you get out of it, so leave that duvet a while before you straighten everything up.

If you are in the market for a new mattress, think carefully about what you buy. Stain-resistant and flame-retardant chemicals are likely to have been sprayed on most mattresses at the factory. Foam cushions are made from petrochemicals and they can give off chemicals over time. Over the course of ten years (the average lifespan for a mattress), a foam mattress loses up to an amazing half of its weight. Think about it – where does that weight go? Unfortunately, much of it goes on your bedroom floor as toxic dust; it also leaches into the air as formaldehyde gas. Think about buying a natural organic cotton or hemp mattress. Alternatively, try a natural latex one.

If you are not yet in the market for a new mattress, think about buying a mattress case and adding a wool, feather or rubber topper to your mattress. It won't stop the chemicals from leaching out of your mattress, but it will put some distance between you and them. Choose pillows and duvets made with organic wool, feathers, cotton, hemp, spelt and millet, buckwheat hulls or natural rubber.

Here's an idea for you...

Help yourself to a restful night's sleep by using organic herbs. Valerian (*Valeriana officinalis*), passionflower (*Passiflora incarnata*) and hop (*Humulus lupulus*) are particularly useful as sleeping aids. These herbs can be bought loose and made into a small sleep pillow made from organic cotton. Breathing in the scent of the aromatic herbs as you fall asleep will help you to rest peacefully so you wake refreshed to face the rigours of modern life. Try herb teas as well; limeflower is traditionally supposed to aid sleep, and chamomile is soothing. You'll probably find some organic blends designed for just this purpose in your local health-food shop.

Don't just stop there – think about your curtains. There are many beautiful organic fabrics which have not been treated with chemicals and they make a great alternative when you are replacing curtains, so do some research online and find a convenient source. Don't forget your bedlinen and towels either; you can do the same for them.

Get a HEPA (high efficiency particulate air) air purifier. A good HEPA filter will remove 99.97% of all particles of 3 microns or larger from your air. I have one plugged in next to my bed and have felt the difference. Use a vacuum with a HEPA filter to clean the bedroom, including a regular sweep under the bed. If you do not use a HEPA vacuum, the dust just moves into the air so you breathe in even more as it whooshes around the room – and it takes eight hours for it to settle again. As in other rooms in the house, use non-toxic cleaners. I like to use organic lavender oil and plain warm water to clean in the bedroom and the lavender oil makes for a calming aromatherapy experience, both when you are cleaning and afterwards – a bargain!

Sleep is the golden chain that ties health and our bodies together.

Thomas Dekker, dramatist

How did it go?

Q. Are organic mattresses going to be as comfortable as high-tech modern mattresses? I've heard that they are rather hard.

A. Organic mattresses actually have some comfort advantages over traditional petroleum-based foam mattresses. They are better at wicking away moisture from your body than foam, which helps anyone who suffers from overheating or night sweats. Wool regulates body temperature very well. It is also resistant to dust mites, which can cause allergies.

Q. I'd like to buy some organic bedding but I don't really have the time to shop around in lots of different places looking for it. Can you buy whole packages from anywhere?

A. Your best bet is to shop online. Not only does this stop fruitless trailing backwards and forwards to shops that do not stock organic bedding in the first place; it also stops having to search in many stores to get exactly what you want. If you search online you will find a variety of organic bedding suppliers close to you. It will also help you to compare prices and products without ever leaving the comfort of your home.

29. Paint it green

We've all thrown open windows to make a 'well-ventilated space' to escape the fumes caused by decorating. Now, at last, there is an alternative!

If you're about to give a room a facelift, what are your greener options?

Conventional paints are made from petrochemicals. Not only are they made from non-renewable sources; they are also responsible for allergy and health problems. That's not only while they are wet and volatile – they also contribute to the general build up of toxins in our homes and workplaces that lead to sick building syndrome and a whole raft of allergies and associated health problems.

The problem is VOCs – volatile organic chemicals. That's not organic in the sense of chemical-free, obviously! Conventional paints are loaded with these chemicals which become gases at room temperature. They include benzene, formaldehyde, toluene and vinyl chloride. Chromium and cadmium are also found in paint pigments. These chemicals are there to make the paint easier to use – it lasts longer, is resistant to fungal growth and spreads more easily. But at what cost?

Exposure to VOCs can cause irritation to your eyes, nose and throat, headaches, skin reactions, vomiting, nosebleeds and dizziness. In the most extreme cases, it can cause liver and kidney damage.

The main culprits

- **Formaldehyde** is a known carcinogen. A common 'indoor pollutant', it is found in everything from the clothes we wear to the artificial-particle wood used in much flat-pack furniture. It is also present in paint. Formaldehyde is an allergen and asthma trigger. Common symptoms of exposure to formaldehyde are watering/stinging eyes, congestion, breathing problems and skin rashes. It can cause flu-like symptoms. Repeated exposure can result in bronchitis.

- **Benzene** is highly toxic when inhaled. It can cause chromosomal damage, and a variety of cancers, including leukaemia. Benzene inhalation can also cause headaches, dizziness and drowsiness.

- **Toluene** is an industrial solvent. It is a neurotoxin and a developmental toxin. If inhaled directly, it can cause headaches, confusion, dizziness and memory loss. If exposed regularly, brain damage can occur. Research suggests that it may also cause liver and kidney damage. Toluene can also be found in drinking water – one reason why old paint should be treated as hazardous waste, disposed of carefully and never, ever, tipped down the drain.

Finding safer alternatives

You can find out the VOC content of any paint by reading the label; it is measured in grams per litre (gm/l) and find the lowest VOC level you can. The safest choice

Here's an idea for you...

Try not to decorate too often, but when you do decorate, help to keep your indoor air clean by adding a few house plants. NASA research found that Philodendrons were among the best house plants for removing formaldehyde from the air (caution if you have small children – they are poisonous so keep them out of reach). Peace lily (*Spathiphyllum* – the same warning applies), bamboo palm (*Chamaedorea seifrizii*), weeping fig (*Ficus benjamina*), rubber plant (*Ficus elastica*) and ivy (*Hedera*) are all good at improving air quality. One plant should be allowed for approximately nine square metres of floor space, so that's two or three plants to impact upon air quality in the average living room.

is to buy no-VOC paint, such as sold by Natural Deco. There are more brands available than you might think, so do some research online. Decorating supplies, including paint and paint stripper, are also available that are produced entirely from natural ingredients such as oils, resins, wax and natural pigments.

Ecos paints produce a great range of products that not only do not contain VOCs – they actually reduce them in your home! The company claims that the air inside your home is up to seventy times more polluted than the air outdoors due to chemicals discharged by carpets, furnishings and paints. Apart from VOC-free paint, they also make a paint containing silicate. They claim that this absorbs and neutralises up to 99% of pollutants in the air of your home. The silicate acts like a sieve, sifting the pollutant VOCs out of the air. Once absorbed, they are rendered harmless. The rub is that this comes at a price. The paint isn't cheap, but in the scheme of things it may be worthwhile spending to safeguard your health. Changing paint seems like a small thing to do but it is these small things that add up to make our lives less chemically overloaded. This paint comes in 108 colours (I was a little worried there would be a choice of white or off-white), so check it out and see if there's anything to suit you the next time you decorate!

Decorate your home. It gives the illusion that your life is more interesting than it really is.

Charles M. Schulz, US cartoonist and creator of *Peanuts*

How did it go?

Q. I've already bought some conventional paint, so what safeguards can I take during my decorating session?

A. Keep your house well ventilated, opening doors and windows. Consider using a face mask while you paint – not a thin paper mask but a plastic mask with filters made especially for the job. Go out for the evening while the paint dries. Best still, use non-VOC paint in the first place, and save yourself from all of these problems. This is particularly true for pregnant women, as the chemicals in paint fumes can cross the placenta and may be harmful.

Q. I have quite a bit of MDF in my house. I'm worried, because I have heard that it gives off formaldehyde. Short of ripping everything out, what can I do?

A. Ecos make a 'passivating primer' that can be painted onto MDF, chipboard and similar particle woods. It absorbs formaldehyde, and can be overcoated with their paint. The paint isn't cheap, but it's a lot cheaper than replacing all of your MDF!

30. The green, green grass of home

Tonnes of chemicals are spread on lawns every year to keep them green and supposedly 'healthy'. They are tracked into the house where residue lingers on carpets and floors.

It doesn't have to be this way — there are alternatives! Maintaining lush green grass doesn't have to mean resorting to a bottle of chemicals...

Walk into any garden centre and you will see a huge array of 'lawn care' chemicals – liquids, powders, crystals – take your pick! It is sobering to stand and think about the sheer volume of chemical that gets sprinkled over lawns every year – and all to make a dull monoculture. If you keep a lawn healthy, it should overcome most weeds (such as moss) itself and be more resistant to drought, pests and diseases. And a lawn with a few 'weeds' such as daisies, speedwell and clover makes for a much prettier view! Clover even helps to feed the lawn as it is a nitrogen fixer; that means it collects nitrogen from the air and releases it from its root nodules, making it available to the growing grass.

I have a lawn. It's left longer than most (when the geese haven't cropped it too closely). To me, a lawn is a flattish open space for recreation. During the day, it's a place for football matches, wrestling, teddy bears' picnics, chasing bubbles and slumping down for picnics. In the evening, it's a place to read (or write!) a novel, accompanied by a generous glass of wine. Think about it. Do a few daisies detract from this type of enjoyment? What is your lawn for? If it's just for looking at, wouldn't you be better off with a flower bed, herbs or a potager packed with vegetables?

Taking care of a lawn organically is not hard. Much of the work is about keeping on top of things so that problems can't develop. Make sure, for example, that you do not cut

Here's an idea for you...
When you aerate your lawn, spread a thin top-dressing of a mixture of leaf mould, loam and sand. Work it into the surface with a broom. Another alternative is to spread a thin layer of autumn leaves over the lawn and mow them well. This chops them up and dresses the grass. Great for lazy gardeners like me who have a tree in the lawn already…

your lawn too short. This stresses the plants and makes them more susceptible to drought. Even if you do not have a hosepipe ban, it is not environmentally desirable to pour gallons of water on an area of lawn just to keep it green.

When you cut the lawn, leave the clippings behind if possible. As they decompose, they release nutrients back into the soil – up to 30% of the lawn's needs. I only remove grass clippings on my first cut of the season and my last, when the temperatures are lower and decomposition is slower. At those points, I mix them into the compost heap. Don't just hurl a big pile onto the top of the compost or it will just rot into a blob of nasty, anaerobic sludge – exactly what you don't want. Mixing is always necessary when adding grass clippings to compost, at any time of the year.

Annual weeds are dealt with by the mower. If you have a problem with perennial weeds, dig them out regularly. Use a narrow trowel, such as a bulb planter, or buy a weeding tool. This helps you to get under the weed and pull it up without leaving big tap roots behind. You can feed the lawn if necessary with an organic fertiliser such as seaweed extract applied in liquid form as a foliar feed (absorbed by the leaves). This will make the grass very green. Don't overfeed, though, as that causes lush growth that's prone to disease. And if you have a problem with moss, aerate the soil beneath your lawn each autumn by making holes in the soil with a fork (it's a great idea, even if you're comparatively moss-free, too). The holes allow water to drain from the surface of the grass, and this helps to prevent moss regrowth.

A lawn is nature under totalitarian rule.

Michael Pollan, writer

How did it go?

Q. I get lots of bare patches on my lawn, courtesy of dogs and kids. What can I do about this?

A. This is not a hard (or uncommon!) problem to deal with. Re-sow the patches in spring. Fork the soil in the patches over gently to break it up. Rake it smooth and sprinkle handfuls of grass seed. Make sure you choose a mixture that is suitable for your particular needs i.e. hardy to withstand heavy wear. If the area is shady, choose a suitable seed mix or you will have bald patches again very soon. Cover the patch with fleece to keep the birds off or you'll end up with fat birds sitting on handy dust/mud patches. Water the patches regularly until they are established – you can use grey water for this.

Q. I've just moved into a new house and the lawn is thatched with lots of moss and dead growth and looks a mess. What can I do to help? I'm worried the grass will be choked by all the thatch!

A. To remove thatch from a lawn, use a spring-tined rake. Draw it firmly across the thatch – it's hard work so you'll need cold beer in the fridge! Rake a small area at a time so you can actually see progress. You can also hire a powered scarifier which may be an option if the lawn is large or very bad. Removing the thatch will stimulate the grass to produce side shoots, which will thicken up your lawn. You can put the thatch on the compost heap (after having a grass fight, natch). In the spring, I leave small heaps and watch the birds collect it as ready made nesting material.

31. Bath-time beauties

Organic bath-time treats contain no chemical nasties and smell great. What's not to like?

Sometimes it's nice to treat yourself and have a splurge on some beautiful bath products.

If I'm feeling in need of being pampered – maybe I've had a hard week at work, or have had hassle with the kids – I like to treat myself to a home spa. I like to make my own bath treats but there are some fabulous products available over the counter now that don't contain parabens, SLS (sodium laurel sulphate), artificial colourings and preservatives. Your skin is the largest organ of the body, protecting your internal organs, helping you to regulate your temperature and eliminate waste products. It's worth remembering that the things you put on your skin are often absorbed by it and enter the bloodstream – so it's vitally important to keep it natural where bath products are concerned to avoid chemical overload. Some experts believe that up to 60% of the materials we put on our skin is absorbed – and that can amount to 2 kg of unnecessary chemicals a year!

Lying in a bath scented with organic lavender oil, or an almond milk soak makes me feel like a goddess – and that has to pay dividends in other areas of life from work to relationships! So what's out there?

Bubble baths

Organic bubble baths usually contain vegetable-derived bubbling agents such as potassium cocoate (derived from coconut) to make suds. They are often scented with organic essential oils and can even have therapeutic effects if created by a herbalist or aromatherapist. Special blends can be used to induce relaxation or stimulation. The addition of natural organic oils and milks act as a moisturiser and make your skin smooth and soft. My personal favourite is Stress Bath Soak from Free Spirit Organics, containing ylang-ylang to create balance, cedarwood and geranium to relax the nervous system and rose oil to soothe.

Bath oils

Organic bath oils do not foam, and most lie on the surface of the water. That means you can enjoy the scent of the oil in the bath water and, when you step out of the bath, your skin is coated in luscious fragrant oil, keeping it supple and healthy. Try bath oils that use sesame or jojoba as a base if you like a lighter oil. Coconut (my favourite – the scent is delicious) or olive are good choices for drier skin. The base oils act as an emollient (moisturiser), soothing and nourishing your skin, and any essential oils added to the mix offer a variety of therapeutic effects. Although I like to make my own oils infused with herbs from the garden, I also love the range of bath and body oils from Hedgerow Herbals – they are a real treat.

Here's an idea for you...

Have a go at making your own herbal oils for the bath. Buy a good quality organic base oil such as olive oil. Decant a little oil into a small bottle and add a few sprigs of your favourite organic herb. If you have herbs such as lavender in the garden, try that for a relaxing, calming bath, and rosemary is great for a stimulating bath to help clarify your thoughts. Pop a couple of sprigs into the oil, screw on the bottle top and leave the bottle in a warm place; after a week, replace the herbs with a fresh sprig. Repeat for three to four weeks for a strongly scented oil. Then add it to your bath-water.

Bath salts

Bath salts used to be the archetypal 'present for granny or aunty' when I was a child, but that sickly-sweet, improbably coloured product is nothing like the bath salts of today. Some of the best are made from sea salt – and even Dead Sea salt for a mineral-rich soothing bath. Mountain Rose Herbs are one company with a wonderful range. I like to use a home made bath scrub made from sea salt, olive oil and my favourite essential oils to exfoliate my body before a bath, but you can buy many wonderful salt scrubs from organic suppliers, such as Daily Body Scrub, White Tea No. 22 containing the powerful antioxidant properties of white tea from the Organic Bath Co. Experiment until you find your favourite.

I test my bath before I sit,
And I'm always moved to wonderment
That what chills the finger not a bit
Is so frigid upon the fundament.

Ogden Nash

How did it go?

Q. So many products profess to be herbal or botanical, with beautiful pictures of plants on the label. When you actually read it, they have a terrifying list of chemical ingredients. How do I know if a bath product is organic and free from SLS and parabens?

A. Always look for organic certification such as that offered by the Soil Association in the UK. Manufacturers are forbidden by law to label a product as organic if it is not certified as such. Failing that, contact the manufacturers and ask! Most truly organic and natural products make it quite clear on their labels or on their websites. If in doubt, always ask.

Q. I have a baby and a toddler, and feed them organic food – so I'd like to make bath time organic too. Can you buy organic baby bath things?

A. There are many companies that make organic baby bath products – especially important for delicate skin and young bodies. California Baby make a lovely range that includes essential oils to soothe cranky babies and even include a bubble wand to play with at bath time. Burt's Bees have a wonderful product called Baby Bee Buttermilk Bath soak, which is free from nasties. Apart from the handy exercise in alliteration, this product contains buttermilk to make your baby's skin soft. Have a look around most baby websites and you will find a dazzling array of products for green babies.

32. Whack those weeds!

Organic weed control can be hard work – covering, pulling, slashing – but there are shortcuts you can take to help you to avoid even a splash of heavy-duty chemicals in your garden.

Weeds are quite literally the bane of my life...

As a long-time organic gardener, my battle against the weeds has left me seasoned, wounded – but (as yet!) unbeaten. We have fourteen acres, and use no chemicals. That means we have extensive experience of weeds in all their glory, from dock and dandelions to nettles and the dreaded couch grass and ragwort. Over the years, we have developed a variety of strategies for defeating these beasts. The most useful is covering them, choking the life out of them by blocking the light they need to thrive.

I have tried old woollen carpet (starting with the ones ripped out of the house after we moved in – we have wooden floors to keep grime at a minimum). In theory this is a great idea; it saves the old carpet from going into landfill, and forms a thick (and free) barrier. Unfortunately, I found to my horror that it held the moisture to such a degree that I was soon hosting slug parties, so the carpet was consigned to the compost heap. This was wool carpet; artificial fibres may contain chemicals that are leached into the soil as they slowly degrade, so use caution.

Back at the drawing board, I considered my options. Using black mulching fabric was my next trial. It lasts for years. Light is blocked, but water can still pass through to your

142

plants' roots. Go for the best you can afford; the cheap soft fabric type I have tried and found wanting. Strong perennial weeds such as dock, and sharp thistles punch through the fabric and weaker but annoying annual weeds such as cleavers soon follow through the holes. I have found the only effective fabric to be the thick woven type bought on a roll. It isn't cheap, but lasts for many years (some of mine is eleven years old and still beating weeds). Buy it in bulk online for cheaper prices and delivery, but shop around. It is worth contacting your local gardening club or allotment society to see if you can buy as part of a group. Online, agricultural suppliers are much cheaper than garden centres, but you tend to have to buy in larger quantities. You could get together with friends, though, and share the cost.

I have also experimented with organic mulches to suppress weeds. I have used thick straw to block the light on ground left fallow. As this rots, it can rob the soil of nitrogen, but as I just dig it in at the end of the season it seems to work. I have had mixed results, but the thicker the mulch, the more effective it is. The cats are very keen on this mulch in particular as it is warm and cosy! The fact that mice nest in the straw is a drawback for me; for the furry girls, not so much.

I have also tried composted bark (pretty good, but expensive so perhaps only useful for smaller decorative beds) and thick layers of newspaper. The idea is that you water it and it forms a barrier, papier-maché style. The reality is that I ended up with sharp hawthorn hedgerows full of paper that took me weeks to put right. I am hoping to try a new material shortly called strulch, which is a composted straw that makes a thick matting once laid. I am a sucker for advertising campaigns that promise less weeding…

Here's an idea for you…
Make friends with your foes. Some common weeds, such as nettles and dandelions, can be used in cooking or herbal remedies. Try nettle as a herbal tea (you may need to add a little honey to give it some taste), or make the smaller top leaves into a lovely green springtime soup decorated with a swirl of crème fraiche. Use dandelion leaves as a salad ingredient – go for the young ones as the older ones can be bitter – and wash them well.

My best friend in the world when it comes to weed annihilation is Sweetpea the goat. I tether her on the patch to be cleared; she happily munches. One hungry goat cannot cope with fourteen acres, however, so I have been trialling a new toy. It's a 6.75 hp commercial trimmer mower, and I'm in love. At the first excuse, I'm out there hacking down weeds taller than me, taking out all of my pent up frustrations. Great stuff! Now, I need a big monster machine because fourteen acres is a *big* garden; you may not need such a macho beast, but the principle is the same. Cut the weeds back before they have time to seed. It weakens them if you keep at it, and stops the seed from spreading.

Finally, compost the cuttings in a separate hot box. You need to make sure it gets hot enough to kill any seeds, otherwise you are adding a whole new crop of weeds to your soil with your lovingly made compost.

They know, they just know where to grow, how to dupe you, and how to camouflage themselves among the perfectly respectable plants, they just know, and therefore, I've concluded weeds must have brains.

Dianne Benson, *Dirt*, 1994

How did it go?

Q. I'd like to try a weed burner. Do you have any tips?

A. Remember that these are primarily designed to be used on hard areas such as driveways and patios. Using them in a field could (apart from being ineffective!) lead to a fire. These work by bursting the cell walls of the weeds and killing them, rather than burning them to a crisp, so read the instruction booklet carefully for optimum efficiency. Of course, weed burners are not the greenest of options and their use may add to air pollution and the increase of greenhouse gases – so composting is a better option.

Q. My dad always poured salt into the centre of weeds. Can I do that in my organic garden?

A. Yes, you can… if you really want to. It is organic, it does kill weeds – but unfortunately it will kill other plants, too, so it is not a great choice. It's a bit like cracking a walnut with a mallet as it also renders the soil under and around the weed useless until the salt eventually disperses, and that may take a number of seasons. You could be storing up problems for the future, so maybe give the salt a miss.

33. Make it natural

A little bit of powder, a little bit of paint... but at what cost? Look closely at what's lurking in your make-up bag.

Do you ever think about what colour cosmetics you are putting on your face beyond whether the colour matches your outfit or eyes?

You may be surprised – or even horrified – when you realise what your make-up contains. Coal tar colours, benzene, even formaldehyde, are just a few of the synthetic chemicals commonly found in everyday cosmetics. These toxins are, of course, absorbed into your skin every time you use conventional eye shadow, foundation, mascara, blusher and lipstick. Although there are only tiny amounts of these substances applied each time, there is the danger of the 'cocktail effect' when a variety of substances are used together – they may interact. Using conventional make-up over the course of decades has a cumulative effect, as well. It has even been claimed that some of the substances confuse hormone receptors and alter cell structure. If you avoid unpleasant chemicals in your diet then it makes sense to also try and avoid them, wherever possible, when you are choosing your make-up.

Think about where and how make-up is applied. Eye shadow, mascara and eye liner is put on in such a way that some of it can actually enter the eye (as anyone with contact lenses can attest). This means it can be absorbed by the very sensitive mucous membranes. Any powders can be inhaled, and they can irritate your lungs. Lipstick disappears off your lips – however thickly it is applied or however many times it is blotted – even long-lasting ones (and ask yourself how they are made to last so long, too). All that lipstick doesn't end up on glasses and napkins either; lots is chewed or licked off and is subsequently swallowed. It is vitally important, therefore, that the make-up you apply is safe, and organic make-up is free from the dangerous chemicals that conventional make-up is filled with.

The alternatives…

There are organic alternatives available for almost anything, and new companies are being set up all the time to fulfil growing demand. A growing number of manufacturers do not use synthetic or petroleum-derived ingredients, GMO (genetically modified organism) ingredients or irradiated products. They use organic ingredients and do not use animal or animal slaughter by-products.

Greenpeople stock a range of certified organic lipsticks, using organic coconut oil, jojoba oil and cupuaçu butter (the produce of a tropical rainforest tree similar to cacao). They are soothing to dry lips, containing organic beeswax, castor oil and myrrh. Nvey Eco UK have a fabulous range of organic make-up with a wide variety of colours. If you carry out an Internet search, you will find many other alternatives available, such as LoveLula, Logona and Suncoat.

Here's an idea for you…

If you find some make-up you think you're interested in, but don't know what colour to go for, ask if they can send samples. This is particularly important when you are buying cosmetics by mail order. It is difficult to get realistic and accurate representations of colours online and you do not want to make expensive mistakes. Some companies will send samples of new products with orders, too – enquire. You won't be the first.

The problem is that, at present, most of this organic make-up is not available in high-street stores, but actually has to be bought online. That removes the pleasurable buzz of looking at new colours and samples, and makes it harder to choose appropriate colours. Life's hard without a range of testers in front of you! However, it's worth it in the long run to know that you have bought quality make-up containing safe ingredients. I make a point of asking where the organic make-up is in shops so that they know there is a demand for organic products. It hasn't worked yet, but if we all ask, we'll get there!

Beauty is about perception, not about make-up. I think the beginning of all beauty is knowing and liking oneself. You can't put on make-up, or dress yourself, or do your hair with any sort of fun or joy if you're doing it from a position of correction.

Kevyn Aucoin, make-up artist and author

How did it go?

Q. I have some lovely sparkly powder eye shadows that I'd hate to get rid of. I'm not sure how dangerous they're likely to be (now I know more about the ingredients in my make-up bag) and I'm not certain if I should just chuck them out. Will I find anything organic to replace them?

A. It's all a matter of choice, really. Some make-up is worse when it comes to dangerous chemical ingredients than other types. Chemicals are transmitted into the bloodstream once they have been absorbed into the skin. Oily creams and lotions allow more of the chemicals to be absorbed into the skin than powders, so your powder eye shadow could be perhaps viewed as a 'best of a bad job' scenario. There are alternatives to non-organic eye make-up, however, free from parabens, phthalates, petroleum- and mineral-based oils, synthetic fragrances, colours and preservatives. Do some online research and you'll find some great sparkly colours.

Q. It seems a bit unlikely that there are really so many dangerous chemicals in cosmetics. Surely they have been passed as safe by all sorts of regulatory bodies before they end up on sale?

A. The United Nations Environmental Programme estimates that there are around 70,000 chemicals in everyday use across the world, and around 1000 new ones are introduced each year. The National Institute of Occupational Safety and Health has reported that around 900 of the chemicals used in cosmetics are toxic. Many chemicals not allowed in food or drugs are permitted in cosmetics – so yes, make-up contains a lot of dangerous chemicals!

34. Botanical beauties

Aromatherapy is the use of essential oils, extracted from plants, to improve your general well-being. Does it have any beneficial effect, or is it just raising a stink about nothing?

Aromatherapy can be used to treat the mind, body and spirit

The use of essential oils in this way is not new. The Egyptians were using aromatic oils in this way 3000 years ago. In the modern era, the word aromatherapy was first used in France in the 1920s. The French chemist René Maurice Gattefossé burned himself badly while working in his perfume laboratory. He thrust his arm into the nearest vat of liquid, which was lavender oil. His burn healed quickly, with no scarring.

In recent years, there has been an upsurge of interest in aromatherapy, along with many other alternative therapies. You can't go into a homeware shop without tripping over piles of aromatherapy candles, and pharmacies and health food shops are piled high with bottles of essential oils. Aromatherapy is one of the most popular forms of complementary therapy and many people buy over-the-counter oils. Health professionals also use aromatherapy therapeutically in a range of settings. But how can it all possibly work?

The link between our sense of smell and the way our brains work is powerful. The limbic system is the part of our brain related to smell and it also deals with memories and emotions. The limbic system influences the endocrine system and the automatic nervous system. It is connected with the nucleus accumbens, which has been called the brain's pleasure centre – which in turn plays a powerful role in sexual arousal and the high obtained from recreational drugs. We know that smells are linked to memories and emotions from our own evocative, if unscientific, experiences. The smell of baking makes us feel comfortable and secure; the smell of spices such as cinnamon and cloves whisks us into a Christmas memory.

The essential oils used in aromatherapy are obtained by a variety of methods. Plant parts are used in a process of steam distillation to extract the oils. Expression is used for certain oils, such as citrus; the oil is squeezed from the peel. Maceration is also used, where the plant material is immersed in hot oil. Finally, enfleurage is used to extract delicate oils by pressing flowers between oiled glass plates.

Here's an idea for you...

To smell an aromatherapy oil, open the bottle and waft it backwards and forwards under your chin. Don't snort the oil close to your nose, or use the bottle like an inhaler, which can be dangerous with very overpowering aromas. If you are choosing an essential oil for scenting your environment for therapeutic effects, don't be bound by the 'correct' oil for alleviating your condition (such as depression or stress, for example). Think about what scent works for you. I find vanilla gives me a great sense of comfort and well-being, for example, and I use rosemary and lavender oils as a pick-me-up when I am feeling flat or drained.

Aromatherapy uses oils in a variety of ways. The modes of application of aromatherapy include:

- Aerial diffusion. This is where your candles and oil burners come in. Essential oils can be used to scent your environment to help to enhance moods and encourage relaxation.
- Topical applications. This means applying the oil (in a carrier oil such as almond oil) directly to the skin. This may be via massage, oil in baths, essential oil compresses, and in creams and lotions for therapeutic skin care. Components of essential oils are absorbed via the skin into the bloodstream. This absorption is why it is important to use organic and wild-harvested essential oils; if there are pesticides in the oil, they will be absorbed by your body, possibly negating the effect of the therapy or introducing new problems as pesticides are absorbed.
- Direct inhalation. Essential oils can be used for respiratory inhalation, to promote decongestion and to encourage expectoration.

Aromatherapy is often used to relieve stress, to promote relaxation and to enhance general well-being. It is also used to relieve headaches, sleeplessness, tension and pain. It is used in sports therapy and even in the holistic treatment of serious conditions such as cancer.

During a consultation the aromatherapist will take your medical history. No aromatherapist will diagnose a condition unless they are medically qualified; you will be encouraged to seek conventional advice from your GP. Once they have discussed your symptoms, they will decide which oil or oils will help. You'll undress to your underwear and lie on a therapy couch, covered with towels, in a warm room. The oils (diluted in a carrier oil) will be massaged into your neck, shoulders and upper back. Some aromatherapists give a full body massage or a facial massage. An aromatherapy massage can last anything from twenty to ninety minutes, and you are likely to feel drowsy after a treatment as it is so relaxing!

A fragrance is like a cat burglar in your brain, it has the key with which to pick the lock and unleash your memories.

Roja Dove, perfume expert

How did it go?

Q. *Are there any side effects associated with aromatherapy?*

A. Essential oils are very concentrated. This means they can cause irritation if applied directly to the skin without dilution. Contact with the eyes will also cause irritation. Some citrus oils can increase the skin's photosensitivity, making it more sensitive to sunlight. Essential oils should not be swallowed or otherwise taken internally except under medical supervision, as they may be toxic.

Q. *Is aromatherapy safe for everyone?*

A. In the main, yes. It is a gentle therapy. Some caution should be used, however. Certain essential oils should not be used if you are pregnant. Some herbs, for example, are emmenagogues – they stimulate blood in and around the pelvis and uterus, and some stimulate menstruation. Other oils should not be used during breastfeeding, if you have asthma or high blood pressure. A trained aromatherapist will know these things; you buying over-the-counter remedies with the aid of a book may not, so always seek advice.

35. Eco-erotica

You worry about what you put in your mouth, but do you think about what you put in other, equally sensitive, places? There's always an organic option...

It takes a very confident person to wave a fluorescent 'rabbit' in the air and ask about its green credentials!

You grow your own veggies organically; what you can't grow, you buy locally and carry home in your jute bags. You have banished SLS and parabens from your bathroom, and your bedroom is safely decked out with organic cotton and hemp sheets. But look at that bedroom closely for a moment – what about those 'playthings' discretely tucked away in the bedside cabinet (OK – or displayed in your bondage dungeon)? How environmentally friendly – and healthy – are they?

You've probably never thought about it, and if you have you've probably not enquired. That's part of the problem. We are still, in the main, a little shy when it comes to talking about sexual activity, so a discussion about safety is just not happening. But think about it for a moment. Chew-friendly baby toys are

Here's an idea for you...

Make your own organic sensual oil blend for massage – and more. Buy an organic base, perhaps sweet almond oil; it's light, easily absorbed, and contains vitamins A and E and omega-3 fatty acids to feed your skin as well as your senses. Jojoba oil is an alternative which nourishes the skin and regulates sebum production. Add drops of musky, spicy oil such as ylang-ylang or heady, perfumed oils such as rose damask. Enjoy!

regulated so that they are safe for use in the mouth, and medical equipment used in the mouth or in contact with other mucous membranes is tested for safety. Sex toys – not so much. But if you buy organic food, organic cosmetics and organic bath products, it makes sense to buy organic sex-related products too.

What's the problem?

Many sex toys are made of PVC, which is cheap and easy to mould into a variety of shapes, but it is quite a hard material, so it is often softened with phthalates. During production and disposal, PVC also releases toxins. Recent testing has found that exposure to phthalates can damage the reproductive system of both men and women, and can even cause cancer. Heat, a long shelf life and the use of fatty substances (such as some lubes) can cause phthalates to leach out of the plastic in large amounts. A study in 2000 found that ten dangerous chemicals were released by the sex toys examined.

Think for a moment about the vast amount of toys that are made cheaply in China which have been recalled recently, all around the world, as unsafe. It is estimated that 70% of the available sex toys are made in China. If it's not safe to put in your mouth, quite literally, just don't go there. The problem is that many sex toys are sold as 'novelties' – so, basically, they are not regulated in the way that they should be.

What's being done to protect consumers?

Not much. Any regulation that is happening is coming from inside the sex industry itself. Some manufacturers are looking at what can be done to make sex toys safer. They are looking at the ways toys are manufactured and seeing what can be learned. The cute 'I Rub My Duckie' vibrator – looking like a 'respectable' rubber duck as it perches winsomely on the edge of the bath – has been phthalate-free from its invention. It can be no coincidence that the founder of Big Teaze Toys, who makes the duckie, used to work as a toy designer for a major manufacturer. Aware of the dangers with chew toys, the duckie was designed to be safe for sex play from its inception.

What alternatives are there?

There are phthalate-free alternatives. One is hard plastic – not flexible, not soft – and, possibly, not very comfortable! Some vibrators are even being made from hardened glass and metal. Glass carries the risk of being scratched during use and causing cuts or harbouring bacteria which can lead to infections. Other toys are being made from softer but phthalate-free material, such as the Vibratex rabbit vibrator (the one made famous on *Sex and the City*) which is now available in a phthalate-free option. It is sheathed in Elastomer, which is hypoallergenic and soft. It is slightly porous and cannot be disinfected, but it can be washed in soap and hot water.

Organic Pleasures is a new breed of erotic supplies store, so check it out online. It sells organic sex toys and products, and all their intimate toys are free from phthalates and PVC. Goods are also environmentally friendly and biodegradable wherever possible, but there is no worthy whiff about the products stocked. Many are handmade by small, independent companies rather than mass produced.

Is sex dirty? Only if it's done right.

Woody Allen

How did it go?

Q. Sounds a bit lame, but I try not to use too many batteries in my daily life. My sex-toy-related guilt isn't some WASP fear of my own sexuality – but I'm worried about all those batteries going into landfill! Any alternatives?

A. Apart from rechargeable devices and batteries, you can actually get solar charged vibrators, and avoid all that heavy battery use. The Solar Vibe is a small vibrator wired to a solar panel… might look a bit weird sticking out of your knickers, flashing in the sunlight, but there you go!

Q. I buy organic food and drink, and organic skin care products – so I'd like to go the whole way, as it were… Can you buy organic lube?

A. You are spoilt for choice; just go online. Sensua make organic unflavoured or fruit-flavoured lubricant; Yes make organic lubricants free of parabens, glycerine, silicones and petroleum products. As glycerine-based products used during sex make it more likely for women in particular to develop candida, that's great news.

36. Feeling seedy?

Why not try organic sprouted seeds? They are easy to grow, tasty and nutritious.

Sprouts may have a 'knit your own lentils' image, but they are really tasty and have the advantage of being extremely good for you!

Have you ever tried sprouts? Not the bog-standard, green at-Christmas-with-chestnuts type, but sprouted seeds in sandwiches, salads and stir fries. Sprouts may seem like a new fad, but they have a very long history. In Ancient China, doctors used to prescribe different types of sprouted seeds for many maladies. In the West, sprouted seeds and raw foods became popular in the late 1970s and early 1980s when people realised their powerhouse potential as superfoods. Of course, the humble 'mustard and cress' we grew (as 'eggheads' in eggshells) when we were children and munched in sandwiches were no more than sprouted seeds – but we've come a long way since sprouted seeds were merely a garnish for an egg sandwich!

Back in the 1970s, I remember my mother sprouting adzuki and mung beans and alfalfa seeds – fairly revolutionary then. Our methods were primitive, but worked. We soaked the beans or seeds overnight and the next morning put them on a tray covered in damp kitchen roll. We rinsed them carefully under the tap for a

Here's an idea for you...

You can add sprouts to more than just stir-fries, sandwiches or salads – though they are delicious in all of those, of course. Think about including them in a tortilla wrap with hummus and a variety of crunchy salad leaves, or adding them to a Chinese-inspired sweetcorn soup just before serving. Mix them with noodles, omelette strips and organic chilli sauce for an improvised Pad Thai… experiment!

couple of days and then had seeds ready for eating. Some people sprout their seeds in jars, but the seeds often go mouldy because of the lack of air circulation and poor drainage. Others use sprouting bags which can be home made (from organic cotton or hemp) or bought. The idea is that you put seeds in the bag and soak it; some people hang it under the tap at the sink. Bags are best for sprouting grains, legumes and larger seeds; I have found small seeds stick to the material and are tiresome to pick off. You have to shuffle the sprouts around as you water them as air flow is a bit of a problem. Over time, the bag looks a bit grubby too.

Today you can buy a variety of purpose-made sprouters which make the whole process easier. Tray sprouters are essentially plastic trays with small holes to allow water to drain through the seeds. Once you've got the seeds or beans in the sprouter, the trays need watering twice daily (running them under the tap is fine). If you have a sprouter with several layers, this allows you to deal with several different seeds or beans at once. This convenience has to be offset against the fact that you need to rotate the trays regularly as running water only through the top means that the top seeds germinate more quickly than the others. Tray sprouters tend to be good at air circulation, so mould isn't a real problem – but be careful to make sure this is the case when you are buying.

You can also buy automatic sprouters (in the sense that they water the crop for you). These are a more expensive option, but make producing quantities of sprouts a possibility. They tend to work by drawing water from a reservoir and sprinkling the seeds continuously or regularly. Unless the water is changed often, it can become dirty – and the muck gets deposited on the sprouting seeds. Top of the range sprouters, such as the Easygreen, produce lots of sprouts, and are easy to clean. You run the sprouter without seeds and the water that mists through the unit disinfects the system. You can also buy add-ons for your system such as an automatic filling system, and an ozonator (which keeps the unit clean and hygienic).

The drawback with these units is the cost. You could buy a hell of a lot of organic sprouting seeds – already sprouted! – for the cost of the unit, and that is why I am a Go-Sprout devotee. For about £20 these sprouters are excellent value. They produce up to 500 g of sprouts per use, and fit easily in the fridge, if necessary, to keep sprouts fresh after sprouting. They don't need daily rinsing either – a real plus for busy (read 'forgetful') people like me! The Go-Sprout is a dual flask system which uses the heat of germination to provide a humidified airflow for the sprouts as they grow. So you soak the seeds overnight, drain them and leave the Go-Sprout to do its thing. It's worth tracking one down, or finding something similar – search online.

Flowers and fruit are only the beginning.
In the seed lies the life and the future.

Marion Zimmer Bradley, author

How did it go?

Q. I don't like all the seed cases that stick to the sprouted seeds. How can I get rid of them?

A. There are two easy ways to remove hulls from sprouted seeds and beans. The first is to swish them about in a bowl of water until the hulls separate and float to the top where they can be discarded. With this method, put the sprouts on a wad of kitchen towel or cloth to drain; wet sprouts rot quickly in the fridge. You can also use a salad spinner to de-hull seeds. Swoosh water through to make the hulls float to the top in the same way as with a bowl. Spin the sprouts to remove water once you've taken out the hulls, and you can refrigerate them straight away.

Q. What sorts of seeds and legumes can I sprout?

A. Many types of edible beans and seeds can be sprouted – but some beans, such as red kidney beans and their relatives, can make you unwell if they are eaten raw. As with any food, choose organic as there is no point in pumping your body full of nutritious foods and adding pesticides as you go; you will negate the benefits. You can buy single-variety seeds and beans as well as delicious mixtures. Seeds include onion, black radish, purslane, birdsfoot, garlic chive and chia. Don't forget grains too – they have a lovely nutty flavour.

37. Just juice

Organic juice. You can buy it in every cafe and supermarket – but have you thought of making your own?

Making your own juice means that you can produce fresh, tasty fruit and vegetable mixes where you know exactly what's included.

Juice bars, with their perky vendors and whizzy wheat-grass blenders are turning up on high streets everywhere. Supermarkets, health-food shops and delis all sell a dizzying array of delicious organic juices with added minerals and spices, but they are incredibly expensive. Fresh, home made organic juice has high levels of nutrients. Shelf-bought juice, even organic juice, loses nutrients at many stages of processing – bottling, storage and heating (to lengthen shelf life) can all deplete nutrient levels. We rather like inventing our own blends in our family, adding herbs (fresh and organic, of course) and warming spices to the mix as we go along.

Why juice?
Fruit juice is a good, quick way to give your body a boost, and a serving of fresh organic juice can count as one of your 'five a day'. It can never replace fresh fruit and vegetables because it does not contain the fleshy parts of the food – or as your granny would call it, the roughage. You need this to maintain a healthy

Here's an idea for you...

You can add lots of things to your juice to make it even more nutritious. Raw eggs (not for children or pregnant women) add vitamin K, beneficial fats and protein, as do ground seeds. These also contain essential fatty acids. Chlorella and spirulina are worth considering. These are marine algae which are high sources of chlorophyll, magnesium and protein. Chlorella even helps to bind to heavy metals and pesticides. For taste, add coconut (contains medium-chain triglycerides) and cranberries. They have five times the antioxidant content of broccoli, so they may protect against heart disease and cancer. They can also help you to avoid urinary tract infections. See what tastes good!

digestive system. But juice can give you a good supply of nutrients in a natural, easy to digest form. Your body has to work quite hard to break down many fibrous fruits and vegetables, and juicing cuts out this 'problem'. Never forget, though, that this 'problem' – the fibre – is what helps to regulate your digestive system and scrapes your colon clean into the bargain. Who needs colonic irrigation?

Fresh organic juice contains many vitamins and minerals – the exact concentration obviously depends on the ingredients. Most juices (especially peppers and citrus fruits) contain high levels of the antioxidant vitamin C, and the mineral potassium – a crucially important part of your diet which helps to counteract the sodium in salty or processed foods. This can help to keep your blood pressure at a healthy level. Carrot juice is a great source of vitamin A, and pumpkin flesh is a good source of vitamin E.

Juice also contains phytochemicals. These naturally occurring plant chemicals have massive health benefits. Lycopene, for example, is found in tomatoes; it gives them their red colour. Studies have suggested that lycopene has properties that help to protect cells against damage; it may even help to guard the body from cancer. Broccoli, peppers, garlic, cauliflower, beetroot and carrots are all great providers of these DNA-protecting chemicals, so these are great choices for a vegetable juice mix. Cabbage juice is also excellent for digestive problems – but use it sparingly at first or you will reap the consequences!

Fresh fruit and vegetable juices are also rich in enzymes. Contrary to popular advertising-driven belief, enzymes aren't just useful for keeping clothes and bathrooms clean; enzymes are the catalyst for many chemical reactions that occur throughout your body. They help you break down and digest food; they help your body to produce the energy it needs to function. Cooking food often destroys enzymes, so the inclusion of raw foods and juices in your diet is vital.

Fruits and vegetables provide another substance vital for health – water. Remember, some of our bodily tissues, such as the brain, are made of up to 80% water. Many drinks we consume every day – such as tea, coffee and some soft drinks – contain diuretic substances that make you go to the loo more frequently and dehydrate you further. Drinking organic juice means that you are consuming a healthy liquid free of dangerous chemicals which will help you to stay hydrated and well.

Start by juicing vegetables or fruits that you enjoy eating when they're not juiced. Listen to your body when juicing and don't add all sorts of ingredients at once because you may spend a long time on the loo; add things gradually, and in small quantities to start with. When it comes to buying a juicer, start with one of the cheaper ones and see how you get on. Some are very expensive which is fine if you are juicing all the time, but it could be an expensive white elephant.

If life gives you lemons, make some kind of fruity juice.
Conan O'Brien, US television talk show host

How did it go?

Q. Can I juice my whole day's supply first thing and then drink it later?

A. Vegetable juice in particular is very perishable so it's best to drink all of your juice immediately. However, you can store homemade juice for up to a day with only a little loss of nutrients. Store it in a glass jar with a tight-fitting lid. Fill the jar to the brim so you exclude air (which allows juice to oxidise and spoil). Wrap it in foil to exclude light and pop it in the fridge. Do note, though, that juice only counts as one portion of your five a day, no matter how much you drink. You need the benefits from the intact fruit and vegetables.

Q. I find the cleaning of the juicer stops me from using it. Any tips?

A. It can be a faff, but if you wash the juicer immediately the pulp doesn't stick on and there's no danger of mould spores forming. An old toothbrush works well to clean the grater part. I take removable parts and stick them in the dishwasher – it works well and sterilises the parts, but make sure your device is dishwasher safe.

38. Hurray for hemp!

Hemp is for hippies, right? Wrong! This incredibly versatile material is about to go mainstream.

What's the first thing you think of if someone says 'hemp'?

My guess would be that you'd think of a crusty old hippie tuning in, dropping out and smoking a fat one. The thing is, industrial hemp isn't the same as marijuana even though it comes from the same family. Tetrahydrocannabidol or THC – the part of weed that has the narcotic effect – is very low in content in industrial hemp, and will not get you high. That having been said, its cultivation was banned in the US by the Marijuana Act in 1937, and that had repercussions around the world. Hemp stopped being an alternative to wood pulp for paper, oils for fuel and manufacturing biodegradable plastics. That left the way clear for the wood pulp and petrochemicals industries.

The ban has recently been lifted in many parts of the world, including the UK in 1993. This is great news for the environment, as hemp is easy to grow (ready to harvest in only a hundred days) and has few pests – so it's easy to grow organically. The plant even leaves the soil structure in a better condition than it was to begin with, as its roots descend into the ground to a depth of a metre. In addition, hemp plants shed their leaves all through the growing season which helps to add rich organic matter to the topsoil.

Try this recipe for delicious hempseed flapjacks. You need 85g organic butter, 60 g organic brown sugar, 2 level tablespoons organic golden syrup, 80 g organic hemp seed, 170 g organic oats. Melt the butter, sugar and syrup in large saucepan. It's better to use a heavy-bottomed pan and a low heat so nothing burns. Add the hemp and oats, mix well and then put the mixture into a greased baking tray, pressing it well down. Bake in a preheated oven at 180ºC/gas mark 4 for 15 minutes or until golden brown; keep an eye on it because it burns easily. When you take the tray out of the oven, leave it to cool for a few minutes then mark the flapjack into the desired portions with a knife. When it's cool and firm, break the flapjack up.

Hemp is incredibly versatile. Historically, it has had many uses. During the reign of Elizabeth I, all landowners had to grow a hemp crop or face a fine; it was needed to make rope and sails for the fleet. The first draft of the American Declaration of Independence was on hemp paper; so were early versions of the King James' Bible. In the nineteenth century, 80% of the world's fabric was made from hemp. Rembrandt and Van Gogh used hemp canvas and hemp-based paints to create their masterpieces.

Today, hemp is just as indispensable. Under half a hectare of hemp, for example, provides the equivalent amount of raw material for paper making as do over one and half hectares of trees. On the same area, hemp can also produce 250% more fibre than cotton and 600% more fibre than flax. Until 1883, up to 90% of paper was made from hemp. Hemp paper lasts fifty to a hundred times longer than paper made from wood pulp. Wood pulping creates chemical discharge, whereas hemp production does not. Hemp is an annual crop, whereas trees obviously take years to grow before they can be felled to make pulp for paper. Hemp is a very strong natural fibre, three times stronger than cotton. It makes great fabric that keeps its shape and is much more durable than cotton. And using 55% hemp instead of 100% cotton to make a T-shirt saves over 375 litres of water. Recent developments in fabric technology have improved the suppleness of hemp cloth, making it soft and comfortable – it looks and feels like linen but is without the associated care problems. The fabric is very porous which allows it to breathe, so it will keep you cool in hot weather. This porosity also keeps you warm in winter, as air becomes trapped in the fibres and warms the body. It's also resistant to mould and dyes easily.

Hemp is also a valuable food, both for animals and humans. Hemp seed oil is the most balanced nutritional oil available. It contains large concentrations of two essential fatty acids (EFAs) and it's been said that hemp foods are the highest source of essential fatty acids in the entire plant kingdom. You can also use organic hempseed in your cooking and load up on the EFAs. I often add a handful to recipes such as pasta sauces, salad dressings and baking.

Hemp oil has also been used as a health and beauty product for centuries; its essential fatty acids penetrate the skin easily, lubricating and smoothing. Hemp oil is an anti-inflammatory and is an effective treatment for dry skin conditions such as eczema and psoriasis.

Why use up the forests which were centuries in the making and the mines which required ages to lay down, if we can get the equivalent of forest and mineral products in the annual growth of the hemp fields?

Henry Ford

How did it go?

Q. *Are hemp seeds really that nutritious, or is it yet another fad?*

A. Hemp – from seeds to oil – is an absolute superfood. The seeds are full of highly digestible protein and high-quality amino acids, which makes them a near 'complete' source of proteins like eggs, quinoa and soy. Hemp oil is packed with EFAs and is a great addition to salad dressings and smoothies. Be careful, though; it needs to be stored in a dark-coloured bottle as it is full of unsaturated fat and goes rancid easily. Try to consume it uncooked, as cooking any oil reduces its nutritional value.

Q. *I've heard that hemp is used to create biodiesel, is this true?*

A. Hemp is an excellent crop for the production of biodiesel and alcohol fuel, which can be made from the oils in hemp stalks and seeds. Hemp produces more energy per acre than other plants grown for biodiesel, including flax and corn.

39. Eco pets

Don't forget Fido or Kitty when you are seeking a more organic lifestyle! From food to bedding, it's all out there.

Our pampered pets are worth every bit of love and care — and let's face it, money — we lavish upon them.

The pet industry is booming, with everything from designer dog clothes to toothpaste for cats. But we don't just need to think about what's good for the health and happiness of the animals in our life – we also consider the impact we have on the planet.

Cat litter

Cat litter is a major source of waste. Much of this ends up rotting in landfill. Now, many brands of cat litter are made from natural, biodegradable materials such as silica and clay, but it is worth looking for the greenest option. Silica has been implicated in the development of cancers in humans, so it may be worth avoiding it in the form of cat litter for your cat's health, and your own. Some cat litters are loaded with chemicals in the form of deodorant and antibacterial treatments, and these can cause allergies in cats – and their owners. Once the litter is used it is, of course, disposed of into the environment. Add to that plastic litter tray liners and bags used to scoop poop, and that's a lot of landfill.

Here's an idea for you...

Instead of buying dubious cheap plastic toys made from petrochemicals and probably shipped halfway across the world, why not have a go at making your own? A small pine cone makes a great toy for cats. They can throw cones around as they are light, and can be tied on a string for easy batting. A bunch of feathers tied on a cord gives hours of fun – as well as being cheap and natural. Why not have a go at making a pull toy for your dog from organic hemp rope or fabric? Give your rabbit some apple twigs from your organic tree (or a co-operative friend's), or a small organic wicker basket filled with treats.

There are things you can do to ensure your cat has a safe tray, and that you are keeping your environmental impact as low as possible. Always make sure that you buy biodegradable, all-natural litter. You could try a wood-based litter. This comes in pellet form and expands to absorb liquid. It is good at absorbing the inevitable smells, too. I use this litter for my many cats as it is easy to compost. I have a special place where I dump my cat litter – a ditch under a hedge my son has dubbed 'cat crap canyon', no less – and you could find a corner of your garden to bury your litter in the same way, secure in the knowledge that it will add to the fertility of your soil. You can also buy cat litter made from corn (try World's Best Cat Litter), cellulose (try Bio Catolet), wheatgrass and wheat, such as Swheat Scoop. The enzymes in the wheat destroy the ammonia-producing smell in the urine so you avoid nasty smells. These natural cat litters can also be used for small animals such as rabbits and guinea pigs.

Animal shampoo

There are a growing number of organic pet shampoos on the market. Cloud 9 Herbal Shampoo is made from rosemary extract and a variety of organic oils including coconut, tea tree, sage, cedarwood and sweet orange. Earthbath produce shampoos and solid bars of shampoo with organic ingredients, and Aubrey Organics produce an organic shampoo with mistletoe, chamomile and yarrow. Like any other product where you have a choice, try them out and see what suits you and your pet.

Food

Some of the cheaper dog and cat foods contain all sorts of dubious looking wiggly bits from the unfortunate animals they are made from. Even more expensive brands contain chemicals either used during processing or ingested by the source animals. Luckily, there are nearly as many organic pet foods available as human foods. Karma Organic Dry Dog Food uses only organic ingredients and the packaging is 100% recyclable. Timberwolf Organics aims to produce food as close to a wild wolf's as possible: Black Forest flavour includes venison, Wilderness Elk contains elk, salmon, millet and sweet potatoes, and Dakota Bison contains – well, bison. Organic cat food and treats are widely available. Natura offers a good range and Yarrah produce a range of organic dry cat food biscuits and tinned meat products.

Piccolo Certified Organic Rabbit Food is a good organic feed based on organic timothy hay. I've found it's better to give small animals this type of pelleted food as with mixes they often become selective feeders and don't get all of the nutrients required. You can, of course, also grow your own organic greens and veggies for your pet in the garden. You can buy organic bird food and treats; just do an online search.

Until one has loved an animal, a part of one's soul remains unawakened.

Anatole France, writer

How did it go?

Q. Are there any organic remedies for fleas?

A. Lots of organic remedies are available to buy, but there are things you can do yourself. Keep your home well vacuumed; if you vacuum up the eggs as they fall off your pet, you will never get an infestation. I also steam clean the few carpets I have on a regular basis, which kills any escapees as well as keeping things fresh. It sounds weird, but give your cats and dogs garlic tablets in their food (their breath tends to be a bit iffy anyway), as it is exuded through the skin and acts as a flea repellent.

Q. I like to use holistic therapies on myself, to avoid chemicals wherever possible. Can these be used on companion animals?

A. Absolutely! Take professional advice for specific ailments, from a qualified practitioner, as you would yourself. Enquire at your veterinary practice for assistance. You can also buy herbal and homeopathic treatments for pets for all manner of minor conditions and care, including worming treatments, grooming, shampoos and vitamins.

40. Smoothie operator

Smoothies are delicious and nutritious – and organic smoothies are even better!

Very Berry, Blue Velvet, Lemon Lovely — it sounds like a menu in a cocktail bar, but these are the names of popular smoothies.

Smoothies – drinks made with crushed fruit and sometimes with other ingredients such as yoghurt – are amazingly popular across the Western world. Britons drank an incredible 34 million litres of smoothies in 2006, and the market research group Mintel predict that consumption will treble again over the next five years. Smoothie bars have appeared in high streets and shopping centres everywhere; supermarkets and sandwich bars sell smoothies: they are big business. That seems like good news, but be careful. Read the ingredients label carefully. Some of these 'healthy' options are loaded with extra sugars and other additives, and many of the most popular brands are sadly not organic. Commercial smoothies can also be very expensive.

Here's an idea for you...

Make your own healthy frozen dessert by freezing your favourite smoothie. You can make sorbet-type treats with all-fruit mixtures, or make a smoothie with yoghurt or tofu for a lovely creamy mixture. You can either make a lolly by pouring the mixture into a lolly mould, or make a slushy. Freeze the smoothie mixture in an ice cube mould, and when the cubes are hard pop them in the food processor; zap until smooth and pour yourself a huge dollop in the knowledge that it is healthy and you are in fact a saintly person for eating this treat. Serve this in pretty dishes and it's good enough for a dinner party.

With blenders and smoothie makers being sold cheaply in supermarkets and stores, there is no reason not to make your own. It's very easy – basically, throw a handful of ice and the ingredients (organic, of course) that you fancy into the blender and press the button. They're a great healthy boost and help you to get your 'five a day' – though smoothies just count as one portion, like fruit juice, no matter how many you have.

Adding goodies

Don't just confine yourself to organic fruit and ice to make your smoothies; there are many things you can add to the mix to make them tastier – and even healthier.

Yoghurt is an obvious healthy extra. It makes the smoothie creamy and silky in texture. Probiotic organic yoghurt is best as it keeps gut flora balanced and helps your body to fight bacterial infections. Soya yoghurt alternatives, such as those made by Alpro, are great for those with dairy allergies, and add to the creamy flavour of the drink. Rice milk may also be used. Acidophilus powder (a probiotic) can be added to smoothies for an extra boost, so it is especially good after an illness or after taking a course of antibiotics. Add a slug of aloe vera juice and give your digestive system a treat. That's great at healing inflamed tissue or helping sluggish bowels to… er… move. It tastes a bit odd on its own but can be disguised easily in a smoothie. Don't give aloe vera to children under the age of twelve, though

The superfood wheatgrass – which has been claimed as a powerful healer and antioxidant – is great as a smoothie booster; as a shot (as it is often offered) it can be bitter. This juice has a strong flavour, so add it to a strongly flavoured smoothie, maybe with fresh mint to help mask the taste. A spoonful of brewer's yeast will add B vitamins and vitamin C powder, especially combined with Echinacea and zinc will help to fight off a cold.

Adding texture

Nuts and seeds not only add flavour to smoothies; they also add lots of protein and essential fatty acids. If you soak the nuts overnight before adding them to the smoothie, you get a smooth creamy texture; doing this also makes them easier to digest. Almonds are a particularly good choice for their 'milky' taste and nutritional value. They are low in saturated fat and contain calcium, magnesium and vitamin E. Brazil nuts are a tasty option, and are high in minerals such as zinc and magnesium. They are also the richest food source of selenium, which is an effective antioxidant.

Rice may sound like a strange thing to add to a smoothie, but it acts as a low-allergen and all-natural 'bulking agent' for those who like their smoothies thick. I add a scoop of cooked rice when a thick 'milkshake' texture is required. Cooked millet may be added in much the same way.

I love fruit, when it is expensive.

Sir Arthur Wing Pinero, playwright

How did it go?

Q. *I love smoothies but I always think of them as a bit of a summer drink, really. Do you have any ideas to make them more cold-weather friendly?*

A. Make a rich red fruit smoothie with blackcurrants, cranberries, apples and raspberries and add some warming spices such as ginger or cinnamon. It's actually very festive for Christmas. Alternatively, make a vegetable-based drink such as tomato and carrot, and add pepper or a dash of chilli. Experiment and see what works best for you.

Q. *I'd like to get into the habit of having a smoothie for breakfast. Any ideas for a good 'start the day' recipe?*

A. This is a great idea., and if you leave the dry ingredients in the blender the night before, it will be even easier. I like breakfast smoothies to be gently flavoured, so they ease me into the day. Banana is good as the base, with a scoop of raw chocolate nibs (shelled and crushed cocoa beans) for flavour and antioxidant value – and the mixture is delicious. Add a handful of oat bran which will give you a slow burn of energy to last until lunchtime. Toasted barley gives a nutty flavour and it has been suggested that it has antiviral properties, so that will help to keep your immune system strong. If you like your smoothies sweet, add a couple of dates or a few raisins – yum!

41. Raw food revolution

Raw foods – hippie fad or superfood secret?

Raw foods are particularly beneficial if they are organic. Foods free from pesticides are healthier per se; organic raw foods are an excellent tool for detoxifying the system.

Raw foodism is a diet that contains uncooked, unprocessed and mainly organic foods. This includes vegetables, fruit, sprouted grains, nuts, seeds and eggs. It may also include fish and meat, as well as unpasteurised cheese, milk and yoghurt. Raw foodists may purely eat raw food, or just try to include as much raw food as possible in their diet.

If you think about it, all animals are raw foodists – humans are the only creatures to cook their food. Early Prehistoric humans also ate raw food. It perhaps makes sense that raw food is more nutritious, as we know that vitamins and enzymes are destroyed by heating. In 1984, Leslie Kenton's book _The New Raw Energy_ was published. It promoted food such as fresh vegetable juices and sprouted seeds and beans, and was quite revolutionary at the time. Today, there are raw food restaurants in many large cities, and raw food cookbooks are available.

Here's an idea for you...

Try some raw chocolate! Raw chocolate is the chocolate bean in its uncooked form. Chocolate is rich in antioxidants and eating raw organically certified chocolate nibs (or powder, or butter) is a sublime experience! Raw cacao is rich in flavonoids, which help the body to fight off allergens and viruses. It's packed with minerals such as iron, zinc and magnesium; it also contains that all-important serotonin, which makes us feel blissed out after eating chocolate – it's not just the taste! If you type 'raw cacao' into a search engine you will find many online suppliers.

Why raw?

There are many reasons for eating raw foods. Food contains enzymes which makes it easier to digest; heating the food destroys the enzymes. Raw food also contains micro-organisms that stimulate the body's immune system and help it to digest food by adding beneficial bacteria to the gut. This helps to promote a healthy digestive system.

Many people believe that a raw food diet gives people clear skin, and gives users more energy. It has been suggested as part of holistic treatment for many diseases such as cancer, chronic fatigue syndrome and immunological disorders. Even if you are not prepared to follow a fully raw food diet, it would be worth including a good quantity of raw food in your weekly meals. Add chunks of raw vegetables such as courgettes or beets to salads; prepare a crudité platter to eat with a bowl of hummus or yoghurt in front of the TV; make sure you include fruit salad in your lunchbox and sprouted seeds in your sandwiches. Adding raw food to the diet need not be difficult or 'worthy' – and can be very tasty – but there are certain foods that should not be consumed raw, such as most raw meat, kidney beans and potatoes.

Thankfully, today raw food is unrecognisable. In restaurants or at home, you can enjoy raw pizzas, quiches, tarts, cakes, pies, curries, breads, pasta – you name it; it can be prepared raw. There are now lots more appliances to help you prepare food at home so that it's raw but interesting. I have a rather pleasingly named

Spiralizer. This is an amazing little machine. It's a bit all-singing, all-dancing in that it has a juicer attachment (I prefer my electric juicer) and a mandolin – not the instrument, charming and fitting with the hippie ethos though it might be, but a kind of slicer attachment. Again, I prefer my food processor. No, the reason I have my Spiralizer is because it makes noodles. Out of raw vegetables, no less! It sounds weird, but try it before you knock it. You can make vegetable 'spaghetti' out of most hard veggies such as carrot, cucumber, parsnip, beetroot, sweet potato, butternut squash and, my personal favourite, courgette. You can make two different sized noodles, and a third blade helps you to make vegetable ribbons. Add pesto to the courgette noodles and you have an unbeatable (and healthy) meal.

Now I'm hankering after a dehydrator. I grow lots of my own organic fruit and vegetables, and I'm a huge fan of fruit jerky – nothing added, no sugar, no colourings – so I want to make my own to support my habit. Dehydrators aren't cheap, but if you grow a lot of your own produce they are great. You can make fruit chips (dried strawberries and raspberries are gorgeous) for yourself and your kids, safe in the knowledge that they are only eating healthy treats. Vegetable 'crisp' type snacks can also be made using a dehydrator, which will help to keep you and yours away from salty, fatty snacks.

Vegetables are the food of the earth; fruit seems more the food of the heavens.

Sepal Felicivant, writer

How did it go?

Q. I've heard of the Paleolithic diet. I'd like to learn a bit more. What does it include?

A. The Paleolithic diet is supposedly based on the diet of our early ancestors, as based on archaeological evidence. It includes wild game, wild fish, eggs, plants, fruit, honey, nuts and seeds. Obviously, be wary about eating any type of raw meat and take professional advice before undertaking any new regime. However, the principles of the diet are worth noting: avoid processed cooked foods as they have limited nutritional value.

Q. Following a raw diet sounds like a bit of a fuss, and I'm not sure if I have the time. Does it take lots of extra preparation?

A. Many things are simple and easy to prepare, such as fruits, salad, vegetables and dairy products. Other foods can take a bit more effort, but with advanced planning it's not too difficult. If you want to prepare any meal from scratch some effort is involved. The use of appliances such as blenders, juicers, smoothie makers and dehydrators can make using raw food easier. Invest in a good raw food cookbook and search for recipes online.

42. Brilliant biodynamics

Biodynamics is a holistic way of growing food which mixes organics with astrology and homeopathy.

But is it premium organic or just muck and magic.

The concept of biodynamics was devised eighty years ago by the Austrian philosopher Rudolf Steiner. Growers using this type of organic system see plants as a living link between the earth, the air and the wider cosmos. It also recognises the influence that planetary rhythms have on plant and animal growth. Stay with me – it sounds odd, but there are many things science is just beginning to understand and recognise which have been common knowledge to gardeners and growers down the ages.

The idea that plants respond to the rhythms of the day, seasons and planets has gradually become more mainstream. We see plants such as morning glory opening and closing at different times of the day in response to light levels, so we know it works. Books about planting with the waxing and waning of the moon have become readily available, so it does not seem a huge leap that a grower or farmer should take note of these influences and use them. Under a biodynamic system, the farm, smallholding or garden is seen as a self-contained, self sustaining mixed unit – no monocultures here! – which blends together animals, crops and environments to encourage wildlife and thus creates a sustainable balance. The grower or farmer develops a close relationship with the land and becomes sensitive to its rhythms and needs.

Here's an idea for you...

Have a go at gardening with the phases of the moon. Many gardeners – biodynamic or otherwise – believe that planting vegetables during specific phases of the moon is beneficial. Planting when the moon is waxing encourages rapid germination and growth. Scientists have investigated this and found that the gravitational pull of the full moon draws moisture from the earth and up towards the surface of the soil – and thus towards the seeds! To have a go yourself, get hold of an almanac.

Devotees of biodynamics believe that the plants we harvest and eat do not just feed us bodily with their leaves, roots and fruits; they also provide us with vitality and life force. Biodynamics recognises that there is a spiritual dimension to gardening. Emphasis is placed on the integration of crops and animals, and the composting and recycling of nutrients in order to feed the soil. Cover crops, green manures and crop rotation are used in biodynamics in the same way as in regular organic gardening.

When plants are harvested, the earth must be fed to give back the vitality that has been removed. In biodynamics, specially developed therapeutic preparations are used to replenish the vitality of the soil, which feed it before it is replanted. All the preparations are used in homeopathic quantities. These include:

- Compost preparations such as yarrow, nettles, oak bark, valerian, chamomile and dandelion. They not only make the heap more fragrant; they also act as catalysts to break down materials and make elements such as nitrogen, phosphorous and calcium available to the plants which are grown in the soil enriched with this compost.
- Horn silica preparation, which is ground silica made into a plant spray to enhance taste and aroma, and to help plants to develop to maturity.
- Horn manure preparation, which is specially prepared manure made into a nutrient rich spray. This is used to encourage seed germination, root formation and shoot development.

Does it work?

Studies have compared biodynamic farming methods to other types of organic cultivation and to conventional, chemically enhanced methods. Generally speaking, yields and soil quality have been found to differ little from those found under standard organic methods – but they do differ significantly from the results obtained using conventional methods.

The use of biodynamic preparations on compost has been examined, and the findings were that biodynamically treated compost contained an amazing 65% more nitrate than untreated compost – making it a power-house of nutrients for the garden. There were also significant differences in the amount of microbial life present in biodynamically managed compost heaps. Higher temperatures were reached and matter rotted more quickly and efficiently than it did in the untreated heap.

Remember, there was a time – and a not too distant time, at that – when organic farming was considered to be a bit weird and hippie-esque. Today, public demand for organic food is massively outstripping supply. Biodynamics addresses the issue of the continuing vitality of the land, and the livestock and plants we grow and farm – and we may well increasingly see its tenets being incorporated into mainstream organic food production. It's certainly worth considering!

Gardens are nutrition for the senses.

Rudolph Steiner

How did it go?

Q. I'm an organic gardener and I'm interested in these ideas, but some of the things I've been reading about sound absolutely barking – herbs stuffed in animal intestines and shoved in the earth and bark in a buried skull… sounds ridiculous! Isn't some of biodynamics just a load of old knit-your-own-lentils with a dash of witchcraft thrown in for good measure?

A. Admittedly, some things do sound weird, but try to take a general overview of the basic ideas that underpin biodynamics. Remember, too, that even simple organic growing was seen as wacky for many years – and now it's mainstream. Listen to your gut instincts, and use the ideas that you do feel comfortable with to enhance your organic gardening techniques. A lot of what might be seen as 'witchcraft' is just good husbandry using the rhythms of the seasons.

Q. I'd like to try some biodynamic compost preparations. Will they be expensive to make?

A. Well, biodynamic compost preparations are added to the compost or manure heap in small quantities, but make the preparation cheaper by growing your own yarrow, chamomile, dandelion and valerian. Just use these to make your own compost activators.

43. Beastly bugs

When it comes to pest control in the garden, organic gardeners don't reach for chemical sprays when the going gets tough – but they still have a whole arsenal of weapons.

In the organic garden, basic housekeeping will help you to avoid infestations with pests and diseases.

Building the soil with leaf mould, garden compost and green manures helps to create strong, healthy plants that can resist diseases and pest attack. Selecting pest- and disease-resistant varieties of plants helps; so does accepting a degree of imperfection in your produce. It never bothers me if a fruit or vegetable is a funny shape, or has a blemish – most of them look great, but I grow food for taste and vitality rather than appearance.

Regular inspection of your plants will help you to nip problems in the bud, and to stop an infestation before it starts. Buy yourself a pest identification book and get a head start – it's easier to deal with problems if you recognise them! Most effective of all, make your garden a haven for wildlife and beneficial insects and animals; they will muscle into your plot and control pests such as slugs, greenfly and snails for you. Use biological controls to control pest problems in enclosed

Try companion planting to deter pests. Plant strongly scented flowers next to edible crops to do this; it confuses them as they find it harder to identify their food by its scent. Carrot root fly can be baffled by planting in this way – I use herbs next to my carrots for this reason. It's also helpful when collecting veggies for the kitchen!

areas such as the greenhouse or polytunnel; buying them for a large area outside would not really be cost effective.

Pesticides actually compound pest problems. They do more harm than good in the garden, and not just because you ingest the chemicals as you eat the crops. Quite apart from the possible health problems that these chemicals can cause, they tend to be non-selective. They kill highly beneficial insects as well as the pests they are designed for and they also kill off the food supply the beneficial insects need to survive – the pests. This may seem to benefit your garden in the short term, but it means the predators that aren't killed by the pesticides will move on as their food supply disappears. As soon as there is a new infestation – and there will be – there's no predator population and you'll be tied into using more noxious chemical sprays to kill the ever more resistant pests…

Insect SAS squad

Certain insects are the bully boys of the organic garden. The following are your crack assassins and should be encouraged at all costs!

- Ladybirds and their larvae are a gardener's best friend. They go through an aphid infestation like a hot knife through butter. Encourage ladybirds by leaving tangles of matted grass and dry vegetation at the base of hedges. Make a ladybird hotel with a wood frame filled with the hollow stems to help them overwinter, and you'll get a head start in the spring.

■ Lacewings. These lime-green bugs have glittering crystal wings and flicking antennae – and look just like tiny fairies! Don't be fooled – they are vicious predators and dispatch aphids with gusto. Encourage them in the same way as ladybirds.

■ Harvestmen look like very leggy spiders, but they differ in basic construction: they have only one body segment. They eat caterpillars, slugs, aphids and other pests. Leave an area of the garden wild and grassy to encourage them.

■ Ground beetles eat the eggs and young of slugs and snails. They hide in leaf mould and rotting matter, so they can be encouraged by mulching thickly around plants.

■ Centipedes. These creepy creatures live in the leaf mould. They are voracious hunters, and devour slugs and slug eggs.

■ Hoverflies. Encourage hoverflies by planting nectar-rich flowers between your fruit and vegetables. The adults feed on nectar, and you want them to stay in your garden and lay eggs. Their young feed hungrily on sap-sucking aphids.

Larger friends

There are larger garden helpers to attract to your garden. Hedgehogs are number one slug-slurpers and can be encouraged by building log piles and by leaving piles of dry leaves at the foot of hedges. Remember, if you must light bonfires (you should be shredding and composting), always check for nesting hogs before you light them.

Encourage birds to live in your garden. A few can be a pest (don't talk to me about the smug wood pigeons gorging on my peas) but in general they are great pest controllers. Feed the birds during the winter, and leave out water. I also leave out nesting materials in spring, such as cat fluff, goat wool, hay and the contents of the family hairbrushes. Nest boxes can also help. While you're putting up boxes, add one for bats. They eat huge numbers of the mosquitoes which can make gardening a pain.

Make a small pond with a stone pile next to it to encourage predators. The pond encourages frogs, toads and newts to the garden – and they eat slugs and snails. It also gives birds and other wildlife water to drink.

Though snails are exceedingly slow,
There is one thing I'd like to know.
If I out run 'em round the yard,
How come they beat me to the chard?

Allen Klein, poet

How did it go?

Q. Do beer traps for slugs really work?

A. They do! These can be filled with beer or a mixture of milk and oatmeal, but remember to empty them on a regular basis. You can also remove slugs by handpicking them from plants (at night with a torch and a 'slug bucket')… An elderly gardener I know always said he was 'teaching the buggers to fly' and sent them winging onto a neighbour's unkempt plot. I wouldn't recommend that, but do make sure you dispose of the collected slugs carefully, or they will find their way home – straight back to your lettuces!

Q. I've heard about a spray called derris. Is it safe to use in an organic garden?

A. Derris is a climbing leguminous plant from Asia. Its roots contain a strong insecticide. Although it has been used in the past as a 'natural' pesticide, it is extremely toxic. I prefer not to use it. Rotenone – the active ingredient – has been linked to Parkinson's disease, and derris will be withdrawn from sale in the course of the next year.

44. Natural nappies

If you have a baby and you're going green, you'll have to think about environmentally friendly solutions to the poop problem. But what about organic nappies – are they worth it?

Most parents today consider the environmental impact of nappies.

Every supposedly disposable conventional nappy that was ever manufactured is still here, mouldering in landfill, taking over 500 years to finally rot away. Each baby uses between 6000 and 8000 nappies before they are potty trained, they make up 4% of household waste (in the UK) costing the taxpayer £40 million each year to dispose of them. That's a lot of crap – literally. As the nappies fester in landfill, they ooze out methane (farty greenhouse gas) and leachate – a rather unpleasant toxic liquid that can contaminate soil and water supplies. Some conventional disposables are incinerated, but that releases carcinogenic dioxins into the air; it also leaves behind ash containing heavy metals.

Disposable nappies even cause concerns on the green agenda because of the amount of energy they take to produce – three and a half times the amount used to make fabric nappies. They use eight times the amount of non-renewable materials and an amazing ninety times more renewable materials than fabric nappies (it's all the wood pulp that goes into their manufacture). So – we've established that conventional, disposable nappies are a bad thing in environmental terms, but that didn't take much brain power. On top of this concern, there are also possibly health risks involved in using conventional disposables.

The bulk of many conventional disposables (about 60%) is made from wood pulp. The rest tends to be made up of a variety of plastics, such as polypropylene and polyethylene. Many also contain superabsorbent materials in crystal or powder form, such as polyacrylate. Long-term studies have not yet been carried out on these gels to examine the effect on your baby's delicate skin, but suggestions have been made that disposable nappies generally keep a boy's testicles at higher than normal temperatures, possibly affecting future fertility. In all, disposable nappies contain up to 200 possibly noxious chemicals – which is quite a cocktail to hold against damp skin for long periods.

Here's an idea for you...

If you are going to use organic nappies, you really need to think about using an organic nappy balm too. Choose a balm that is free from parabens and sulphates. These ingredients have been implicated as carcinogens, and the moist warm environment of a nappy is conducive to the skin absorbing all manner of nasties. Pur Babies produce a 100% organic nappy balm that contains organic calendula and chamomile to sooth your baby's delicate skin; Natural Child produce a balm made with organic olive and macadamia oil. Have a look around and find one that suits you.

The alternative options...

Organic disposables still end up in landfill, and even though they are biodegradable, they take a long time to break down. They are unbleached, use and expose babies to fewer synthetic materials. They use non-chemical absorption to keep your baby dry, so they may be a viable option if you are travelling, for example.

Moltex OKO disposable nappies are a 'greener' option; they are compostable, biodegrading within eight weeks in an earthworm composter. The cellulose pulp inside the nappy is unbleached, and contains no perfumes or lotions. It is certified as TBT (Tributyl Tin – found in conventional disposable nappies) free, and contains tea-leaf extracts. It does, however contain a small amount of absorbent gel.

Then there are organic reusable nappies. Cloth nappies can be washed and reused hundreds of times (more than enough for two kids), they reduce nappy rash and represent a much better use of the world's resources by minimising waste. White cotton nappies look lovely, but they get to be white through the use of strong – and potentially toxic – chemicals. According to the Soil Association, the conventional cotton farmer uses around 150 g of pesticides to grow the cotton required for one T-shirt. The chemicals cause pollution in the environment, and health problems for the growers. Many parents are choosing organic cotton nappies to avoid any exposure to these chemicals.

Organic cotton is grown using natural fertilisers, compost and the use of chemical free pest control; it's not weakened by chemical treatments, and is soft and strong. Organic cotton velour, such as offered by Swaddlebees, is even softer. Another option is an organic hemp or an organic bamboo terry fabric. This fabric becomes softer the more it is washed, and has natural antibacterial properties. Bamboo fabric is 60% more absorbent than cotton.

Cloth nappies help prevent nappy rash, aid walking and early potty training and are much better for the environment. What are you waiting for?

Arabella Greatorex, owner of The Natural Nursery

How did it go?

Q. I'm happy to use organic fabric nappies, but would like to use a nappy service. Are companies available to wash nappies organically?

A. Some nappy services do provide organic nappies and washing facilities, but you will have to enquire in person locally to find out what is available nearby. If you cannot find a service that offers organic alternatives, consider buying your own organic nappies and wash them in organic soap, or using wash balls. With modern washing machines and a sealed-top sanitizer, washing nappies need be no worse than changing a cat litter tray!

Q. I am pregnant and have made the decision to buy organic fabric nappies for my baby. Where can I find organic pants to cover the nappy and avoid leaks?

A. Organic wool pants are a great option. They are breathable, unlike conventional cotton pants, so promote healthier skin and help to avoid nappy rash. They also wick moisture away from your baby's bottom. You should be able to find some with a little online searching.

45. Conscious cotton and brilliant bamboo

Is the growth in organic clothing ranges just another fad – or a real way to make the earth a healthier place to live?

Time to experience organic clothing at its best.

Synthetic fabrics are made from petrochemicals, a non-renewable resource; these fabrics pollute the environment as they are manufactured, and they make clothes which fade and get smelly really quickly!

Even 'natural' fabrics have their challenges. Growing conventional cotton crops for use in the clothing industry involves massive amounts of chemicals. Spraying chemical toxins is commonplace in conventional growing, to kill insects and weeds in order to maximize productivity. This affects the earth, as many beneficial insects and animals are poisoned (to say nothing of land and water contamination). It also affects the health of the cotton growers – some of the poorest farmers and workers around the world. Pesticide poisoning is responsible for 20,000 deaths and three million non-fatal poisonings every year, worldwide.

On top of that, there are long-term health effects for cotton farmers and their families including breathing difficulties, cancers and reproductive disorders. Chemicals are even used to scour off the waxy outer layer of the cotton fibre to allow dye retention, and raw cotton is bleached white with chemicals like chlorine. Think about it: it takes a substantial amount of chemicals to make one standard T-shirt. How much do you want that cheap T-shirt for your holidays? Better to think in terms of the real, rather than the monetary, cost – and you just might put it back on the rack. You don't have to sacrifice the health of the environment and the cotton producers to wear great clothes; these days there are many alternatives available.

The benefits of organic cotton

Cotton is a difficult crop, prone to disease, but it is now being successfully grown organically – and is making a healthy profit. Organic growing techniques involve crop rotation, which encourages biodiversity; they also give the cotton producers access to more of their land for food crops rather than planting cotton throughout to maximise their (poor and unfairly traded) profits. Soils are fed with organic matter, including manure, which helps to avoid potential soil erosion.

Here's an idea for you...
There has recently been a resurgence of interest in knitting your own jumpers and other garments. Why not have a go, but use one of the delicious organic fibres available – from merino wool to alpaca, angora, bamboo and hemp? Find out more about what is available (in a myriad of gorgeous colours) at suppliers springing up to meet demand, such as Garthenor Organic New Wool, Myriad, Eweporium Organic Fiber Arts, Shetland Sheep & Angora Rabbitry.

Bamboo – the new wonder fabric?

When you think about bamboo, you probably see pictures of garden canes, trendy gardens filled with pagodas and water features – or possibly a munching panda. These days, bamboo is a hot new organic fabric trend, which is great news as it is one of the fastest growing, most vigorous plants in the world! It is rarely eaten by pests and its naturally antifungal properties protect it from disease. In France, *Le Monde* is calling it 'a textile revolution'. Amazingly, bamboo makes a cashmere-soft (but incredibly durable) fabric, due to the round fibres it produces. Its smooth feel makes it great for allergy and eczema sufferers as well as babies and young children.

Bamboo fabric is breathable, and wicks away moisture from the skin – making it ideal for sportswear. It's actually three to four times more absorbent than cotton. In hot conditions, bamboo is cool to the touch but it's also warm and cosy in cold weather, because warm air gets trapped next to the skin, insulating it from the cold. Bamboo garments protect against harmful UV rays, giving a reduction of 98% of rays reaching the skin where covered by the fabric.

Fabric made from bamboo is also antibacterial and antifungal (again – great for producing non-stinky sportswear!). Scientists examining bamboo found it contained a bacteriostasis bio-agent that they named 'bamboo kun'. This natural feature is retained when the fibres are made into fabric – which gives it a naturally built in deodoriser. In tests by the Japanese Textile Inspection Association bamboo fabric still retained these properties even after going through the washing machine fifty times.

If most of us are ashamed of shabby clothes and shoddy furniture, let us be more ashamed of shabby ideas and shoddy philosophies... It would be a sad situation if the wrapper were better than the meat wrapped inside it.

Albert Einstein

How did it go?

Q. I've noticed that organic labels are even starting to appear in large chains and supermarket clothing ranges, but where can I find a bit more variety – and style?

A. There are lots of organic clothing options and some manufacturers are producing only organic clothing ranges. Planet Earth created the Green Label clothing range, which launched in November 2006. This is a far cry from the hippie garments envisaged by many when considering organic clothing. It's aimed at the young, urban male and the clothes are manufactured from organic hemp, cotton, ramie – and even recycled materials. Other suppliers of organic clothes include the Hemp Trading Company, who produce hemp/organic cotton blend T-shirts with hip hop and drum and bass inspired designs on the front – as worn by Goldie, Skinnyman and DJ Hype. Greenfibres sell sumptuous silk and cashmere undies as well as a good range of organic everyday wear; they also carry cute organic clothes for children with barely a beige item to be seen!

Q. How do I know that the clothes I buy with 'organic' on the label are truly organic? Are there rules and regulations in the same way as there is for food?

A. You are right to be wary – some manufacturers are cynically jumping on the organic bandwagon and trying to make items seem better than they are. The UK's Soil Association has produced new guidelines for this growth area, and clothes that display their symbol will have met a number of rigorous standards.

46. Love your shed

Do you ever wish you had a little quiet space, just for yourself, away from the rigours of family life? Then get ahead with a shed!

Here's how to go about making a garden shed into an urban oasis.

A few years ago, like many people who work from home, I built a shed in my garden as office space. Basically, it's a large shed, painted green to blend in with the garden. I've been planting lavender under the windows and climbing roses are ready to go in as I write. It's a gorgeous, airy and light space in the summer, surrounded by birdsong. Dragonflies and butterflies flit past the window then, too… it's idyllic. I only use my shed in the summer as it gets cold where we live, but other writers I know use them all year. With internal wall cladding, the addition of insulation and a gas heater, sheds become cosy nests even in winter. Heavy-gauge, purpose-bought garden offices are, of course, warm in winter – but it is glorified (and affordable!) sheds we are discussing here.

If you are thinking about buying a shed/den, consider buying a purpose-built shed or bog-standard shed kit from a DIY warehouse and adapting it as your own. Check that you are buying an untreated wood shed rather than a pressure-treated one as there may be all kinds of chemical nasties waiting to leach out into your air space (and the untreated ones are usually cheaper too). My shed started out as 'off the peg'. With the addition of heather brush on a roll on the roof it looks more 'rustic', and I plan to nail slabwood (the planings covered in bark left behind when the sawmill cuts a tree into planks) to the outside. This will help to insulate and weatherproof the shed as well as making it into a more aesthetically pleasing hobbit hole. Fix a layer of Perspex on the outside of the glass windows and you immediately have double glazing which will save energy, keep you warmer and keep out noise from traffic and playing children!

Green houseleek can be used as an environmentally friendly roofing material. It absorbs chemicals and looks wonderful; it even attracts beneficial insects to your plot as well. Sedum is a food source for butterflies, bees and many other insects, and gives them a safe place to overwinter. Birds feed on the insects and plant seed heads, and use the dead stalks and flower stems as nesting material. Using sedum roofs helps to increase biodiversity, and it absorbs carbon dioxide – thus helping to reduce global warming. The plants improve air quality by releasing oxygen, and help to filter dust and pollutants from the air. After seeing sedum 'living roofs' at a local garden show, I plan to install one to my own shed.

Here's an idea for you...

For extra organic credentials for your shed, and to make it look really cosy, consider building window boxes both inside and outside. The outdoor ones can be filled with herbs such as creeping thyme, and edible plants such as tumbler tomatoes and cut-and-come-again salad leaves. Inside, use air-cleaning plants such as pothos, philodendrons and spider plants (good at removing formaldehyde from the air). Gerbera daisies are bright and cheerful, and those are good at removing benzene. Make your window boxes from untreated timber and paint them with some organic paint. Add a few broken crocks for drainage, fill with organic compost – and you're away.

Once you have your shed built, make sure you choose natural organic furnishings for the inside. A Lot of Organics (www.alotoforganics.co.uk) is a UK-based search engine set up to find organic options for everything from rugs, organic cotton and wool cushions and curtains to organic furniture. Check it out, or find a local equivalent, to find a range of online stores where you can find everything you need to fit out your organic nest.

Nature is my manifestation of God. I go to nature every day for inspiration in the day's work. I follow in building the principles which nature has used in its domain.

Frank Lloyd Wright

How did it go?

Q. I want to paint my shed – not only to make it last longer, but also to make it attractive. Most of the preservatives for outdoor wood that I have seen are full of harmful chemicals, which kind of defeats the object of a healthy outdoor space. Are there any organic options available?

A. There are organic paints available for both the inside and outside of your shed. Search online but check out real shops as well as virtual ones. Make sure you ask at your local DIY store for organic paints as they may have a range available. If they do not, and if enough people ask, they will know that there is a demand – and this may change their buying patterns. Consumer power drives change in retailing, so make your voice heard!

Q. I'd love a quiet, calm space to call my own so I can work from home. I'm in the UK. Would I need planning permission to have a shed used as an office in the back garden?

A. It's not very likely, but may be worth a phone call to your local planning department to check for sure. You don't want to be settling down cosily in your new den only to find that there's an official knock on the door bringing bad news! You will need to apply for planning permission if any of the following applies: more than half the area of your garden would be covered by the shed; if your house is a listed building, a conservation area, a National Park or an Area of Outstanding Natural Beauty and your planned shed has a volume of more than ten cubic metres; the shed is not to be used for domestic purposes, but for running a business.

47. Fabulous floors and furnishings

You've brought home your organic food, carried it into your kitchen which is painted with organic paint – but what about the table? Does that need to be organic too?

Just when you thought it was safe – you start reading articles about VOCs in furniture.

Emissions of VOCs (volatile organic compounds) from different types of furniture coatings have been investigated to see how they affect air quality in the home. Solvent residues and chemicals given off by varnishes, glues and paints suggest that furniture may contribute significantly to indoor air pollution.

Formaldehyde, for instance, is a commonly used chemical in furniture. It is found in many furnishings, so concentrations in the air become high and create a toxic environment. Some people are more sensitive to the effects then others and children are especially sensitive. Symptoms of exposure may include headaches, breathing problems, disturbed sleep and allergy symptoms. More people are thinking about buying organic furniture to avoid exposure to harmful chemicals – but what are the options?

Organic furniture

A growing number of companies are producing organic ranges of furniture and furnishings. Furnature supply a range of organic mattresses, bedding, fabrics and organic, sustainably produced furniture. The cotton used in the manufacture of its range is organically grown hand-picked cotton from the Peruvian Andes and the wool is from sheep raised organically on a small island off the coast of the Netherlands. The rubber used for mattresses is a renewable resource and comes from a plantation in Malaysia. It is flexible and resilient, and allows air circulation. They use only organic, unfinished wood, and their furniture is made from woods such as spruce, poplar, ash and maple that don't require treating with harmful substances to look beautiful. They use no synthetic glues, sprays or dyes.

Here's an idea for you...

Why not refinish and repurpose some old furniture yourself? I have refinished old furniture from coffee tables to filing cabinets by a mixture of painting and decoupage. I like 'shabby chic' so I don't rub down the furniture first. If you do, make sure you wear a face mask and work outside to avoid any potentially toxic dust. I paint the furniture with organic paint, and add decorations with safe glue such as paste. Pressed flowers, mulberry paper and tissue can all be used to great effect.

There are many other organic furniture suppliers. Earth Friendly Goods produce organic, environmentally friendly furniture including complete bedroom sets, individual pieces and natural latex mattresses. Greenwoods Furniture create a range of furniture made from organic hardwood frames, such as armchairs upholstered with sumptuous, vegetable-dyed leather.

Reclaimed furniture

Increasingly, furniture is being manufactured from reclaimed timber. However, be careful that the furniture has not been treated with chemical finishes. Reclaimed furniture offers a green alternative by making items from reclaimed wine and

whisky barrels, beams and barn timbers. Reusing old timber makes attractive rustic furniture and repurposing old wood helps to save living trees from being processed into timber. An old building such as a warehouse with 300,000 board metres of reusable timber can offset the need to harvest over 400 hectares of forest! Reusing wood also means that it does not end up in landfill sites. Eco2you make a lovely range of chunky furniture using reclaimed roofing beams, sanded back to reveal pine underneath. The furniture is finished in a natural wax and polyx oil.

For inspiration, check out Whit McLeod – furniture in an Arts and Crafts style from salvaged oak wine casks, which gives the furniture lovely patina. Mark Dabelstein's Pallet Art is a brilliant range of items which started from making furniture made from – you guessed it – old pallets. His cabinets are furniture as art. When you open the door, decorative cut-outs of fish, stars and other shapes swing in and out. All the furniture is made from recycled timber and organic paints and finishes.

Organic floors

It stands to reason that when thinking about 'greening' your home, you should consider flooring choices carefully. The floor is a large area, and if it is covered in material that gives off toxic fumes, you are exposing yourself to a lot of air pollution.

Think about choosing natural materials, such as wood and cork. Cork is a great insulator and ensures that minimal heat is lost. Cork's spongy texture also provides excellent noise insulation. Cork is low in VOCs, but it's imperative that any sealer used is chosen carefully. This also applies to wood finishes.

Carpet is warm, so it offers high levels of energy conservation. Caution is advised in this choice because conventionally produced carpets give off high levels of VOCs. Hydrocarbons, CFCs, benzol, vinylacetate, formaldehyde and butadiene are used and produced in the manufacturing process, all contributing to indoor air pollution. Glues used during fitting are also an issue. If you are going to be choosing carpet, go for natural (preferably organic) wool. It is hardwearing, and naturally fire retardant. It is also a renewable resource, and is compostable at the end of its lifespan.

To me a lush carpet of pine needles or spongy grass is more welcome than the most luxurious Persian rug.

Helen Keller

How did it go?

Q. I don't want to use wood or cork, but fancy a natural floor covering like sisal. Are they practical?

A. Sisal is a great choice for floors as it is hardwearing and looks great. It is made from a subtropical cactus-like plant. The fibres are fine and may be woven closely; they also accept natural dyes easily. It's not absorbent, which makes it a great choice for areas that might otherwise get dirty. There are lots of other natural floor coverings, too. Choose from seagrass, coir (from the inner husk of coconuts), mountain grass and jute. Make sure the products you choose are organic – although they look it, 'natural' floor coverings are not as green as they might be. Ask suppliers and use that consumer power.

Q. I saw some lovely hand-made rag rugs recently made from organic cotton. I loved them but they were really expensive. Any ideas where I could find patterns and instructions to make my own?

A. Look for a rag rug course (check online for something close to you); alternatively check out craft books from the library. 'Clippy mats' are both easy to make and practical; basically you hook strips of fabric through a hessian backing and trim the pieces. Go for organic fabrics and you're on your way!

48. Eggstra special – organic eggs

Organic eggs – expensive, but worthwhile in terms of taste and animal welfare. But is everything as 'green' as it seems down on the farm?

If you looked at egg boxes in the supermarket, you'd think all hens lived in happily rustic conditions, trotting about the farmyard. Sadly, this is far from the case.

Most of us know that battery farming is just plain wrong, with hens hemmed in and de-beaked, living in the dark. Galvanised into action by news items and TV programmes, consumers have moved in droves to buy free range eggs. But what does that really mean?

'Free range' animal husbandry, in the eyes of the consuming public, allows the animals as much freedom as possible to live as they would naturally. In practice, there are few regulations imposed on what can be called free range. Beware of meaningless terms made to sound rustic such as 'pasture-raised', 'grass-fed' and 'humanely raised' – they have no legal standing – and alternative terminology can

Have you ever thought of keeping a trio of hens in your garden? If you don't keep a rooster, there is no noise to disturb the neighbours. Hens are easy and cheap to keep, and collecting warm eggs is a delight not to be missed. They help to clear pests from the garden, too. Scout about and see if there is an allotment association near you – many of these include hen keepers. They will be only too glad to give you advice and may even be able to sell you a few surplus pullets. Your chicken house can be cheap and home made (there are many patterns online) or top of the range – your hens will be happy in either!

even be used to make traditional high-density confinement seem humane. 'Cage-free', 'free roaming', etc., can in reality describe high-density floor confinement, with many hens crammed into a barn where they can technically move about, if they cannot do so in reality. In the EU, egg production is classified into four categories: organic, free range, barn and cage. There is mandatory labelling on egg shells which includes a number to correspond with each of these categories: 0 for organic, 1 for free range, 2 for barn and 3 for caged birds.

So how can you be sure about the welfare of the bird that produced the meat or egg on your plate? Simple: only buy organic eggs. Apart from the higher quality of the produce, there are also high standards of animal welfare in operation when eggs are certified as organic. The UK Soil Association's mark is one of the best indications of animal care, with only 500 hens per flock, continuous daytime access to open-air runs with organic pasture, the provision of shelters and drinking troughs evenly distributed throughout the run, with at least four shelters per hectare. From January 2008, Soil Association standards require at least four square metres of shelter on the range for every 500 birds. To qualify for Soil Association certification, hens must also be fed on at least 80% organic non-GM feed.

If hens are kept in large numbers, even with access to the outdoors, the ground can become bare and harbour diseases. To prevent these problems, the ground needs to be rested. The Soil Association requires that land is rested for a whole year after every three years of being stocked with hens. Soil Association meat flocks are usually kept in mobile hen houses, which can be moved about to give the birds fresh grass and to prevent diseases building up.

The Organic Farmers and Growers group is less stringent than the Soil Association, and allows organic certification for flocks of up to 7000 birds. They argue that the Soil Association standard of up to 500 birds per flock would put up to 90% of free range units out of business. As Soil Association organic farmers have to go further, it costs more to raise their hens. In the UK, currently only 30% of organic chicken meat and 7% of organic eggs are Soil Association certified. They are slightly more expensive, but it is worth considering buying them in terms of animal welfare alone. Other organic certifiers with particularly high standards of animal welfare include the Biodynamic Agriculture Association (Demeter) and the Scottish Organic Producers Association (SOPA), and other local organisations exist, so do some research if these aren't relevant to where you live.

Regard it as just as desirable to build a chicken house as to build a cathedral.

Frank Lloyd Wright

How did it go?

Q. I bought some organic eggs last week and when I used them, the yolks seemed a bit pale. Does that mean they are less nutritious?

A. Not at all! The rich, orangey yolks found in many conventionally produced eggs are created with colourings and chemicals. Many hens are given feed containing artificial colouring so the eggs look 'heartier' – and it's what we have come to expect. Not only are organic eggs better for you in terms of being free of nasty substances, and more ethical, it's also been suggested that they are more nutritious. They have been found to contain higher levels of omega-3 fatty acids due to the healthier, more varied diet of the hens.

Q. I think that I read that hens were originally jungle dwellers. If so, wouldn't it be more humane to keep them in wooded areas rather than pasture, to mirror their natural habitat?

A. This is true, and hens are at their happiest in runs that contain trees, hedges and artificial cover to make them feel safe from predators. Soil Association standards require hens to have enough cover including vegetation in their free range areas to imitate their natural habitat. They like to scratch and forage so access to pasture with cover is ideal. My hens are very happy when roaming round the orchard, with the added bonus that they dispose of lots of pests – such as slugs.

Organic directory

If you find something you like the look of on one of these websites, but the supplier can't send it to you or you'd prefer not to have things shipped some distance, then use the sites to inspire you, and find a more local alternative. Use them as inspiration. You don't want to do your best to be organic in some ways, while notching up those air miles.

GENERAL

The Soil Association
www.soilassociation.org
The UK's organic-certification body

Ethical Superstore
www.ethicalsuperstore.com
Large range of products, including cleaners

A Lot of Organics
www.alotoforganics.co.uk
Search engine for organic options

FOOD AND DRINK
Food
Montezuma
www.montezumas.co.uk
For organic chocolate

Purely Raw
www.purelyraw.com
Ready-made raw food online

Detox your world
www.detoxyourworld.com
Organic foods including raw cacao

Sprout people
www.sproutpeople.com
Everything you need for sprouting seeds

Water
Highland Spring
www.highlandspring.com
Natural mineral water is bottled in its natural state, without treatment.

Detox.co.uk

www.detox.co.uk

'Top of the range' water filters

Tea and coffee

Choice Organic Teas

www.choiceorganicteas.com

A wonderful range of different tea blends

Clipper Teas

www.clipper-teas.com

A great selection of teas

Mountain Rose Herbs

www.mountainroseherbs.com

A good selection of organic herbal teas

Coffee Kids

www.coffeekids.org

This charity works with coffee-farming families

Beer, wine, spirits

Real Ale

www.realale.com

Organic, vegan, vegetarian and traditional real ales by mail order

Bonterra Wines

www.bonterra.com

Festival Wines

www.festivalwines.co.uk

Biodynamic, organic and vegan wine

Pageant Wines

www.pageantwines.com

Organic and biodynamic wines

Vine Organic

www.vineorganic.co.uk

Sells a great range of wines and ciders by mail order

Vintage Roots

www.vintageroots.co.uk

Organic wine merchants

Vinceremos
www.vinceremos.co.uk
Organic wine merchants

Cookery and recipes
Penrhos Court/Greencuisine
www.greencuisine.penrhos.com
Organic cookery courses

Cookus Interruptus
www.cookusinterruptus.com
Short DIY videos that show viewers
how to cook fresh local organic
whole foods

Gone Raw
www.goneraw.com
Amazing recipes – 1880 at last
count – including truffles, apple
cinnamon ice cream, chocolate
brownie swirl roll…

Flowercarole.com
www.flowercarole.com
Many fruit recipes

Juiceland
www.juiceland.co.uk
Vegetable recipes

GARDENING
Pondalgae-greenclean
www.pondalgae-greenclean.co.uk
Pond solutions

Rocket Gardens
www.rocketgardens.co.uk
Excellent range of young organic
plants including whole veggie plot
boxes

Growganic seaweed extract
www.growganic.co.uk

Garden Organic
www.gardenorganic.org.uk
Organic gardening organisation,
formerly the HDRA; organise the
Heritage Seed Library (HSL)

Organic Gardening Catalogue
www.organiccatalog.com
A fantastic source for organic seeds
and gardening products

Grow Your Own magazine
www.growfruitandveg.co.uk

The Kitchen Garden magazine
www.kitchengarden.co.uk

Enviromat
www.enviromat.co.uk
Sedum 'living roofs' for sheds and
buildings.

Biodynamics
www.biodynamics.com
A great place to get an
understanding of the ideas and
concepts involved

Herbs
Organic Herb Trading
www.organicherbtrading.com

Supply dried herbs, essential oils
and much more – and all produce
is certified as organic

Hambleden Herbs
www.hambledenherbs.co.uk

Baldwin and Co.
www.baldwins.co.uk

The Herb Patch
www.herbpatch.fsnet.co.uk
Herbs supplied in person or by mail
order

HOME
Cleaning
Natural Collection
www.naturalcollection.co.uk
Planet Pure and Natural House
products

Faith in Nature
www.faithinnature.co.uk
Clear Spring Collection

Ecover
www.ecover.com
A range of washing liquids, powders, cleaning products and dishwasher salts

Sonett
www.sonett.co.uk
Manufacture a range of organic washing products, including washing liquid

Soapnuts
www.soapnut.com
Brilliant, completely natural product

Furniture
Furnature
www.furnature.com
A range of organic mattresses, bedding, fabrics, and organic, sustainably produced furniture

Earth Friendly Goods
www.earthfriendlygoods.com
Organic bedroom sets, individual pieces and natural latex mattresses

Greenwoods Furniture
www.greenwoodsfurniture.co.uk
A range of furniture made from organic hardwood frames

Eco2you
www.eco2you.co.uk
A lovely range of chunky furniture using reclaimed timber

Whit McLeod
www.whitmcleod.com
Furniture from salvaged oak wine casks

Mark Dabelstein's Pallet Art
www.palletart.com
Brilliant range – furniture as art

Celebrate the Seasons
www.celebratetheseasons.co.uk
Craft site; includes step by step description of how to use decoupage to reclaim old furniture

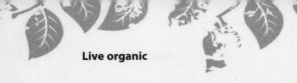

Bedding
Organic Grace
www.organicgrace.com

Luma
www.lumadirect.com

ABACA Organic Living
www.abacaorganic.co.uk

DIY and paints
Ecos Organic paints
www.ecosorganicpaints.com
Carry a range of organic paints,
including a shed and fence
treatment

Natural Deco
www.naturaldeco.co.uk
Paints and finishes

Flooring
Organic and Healthy
www.organicandhealthy.com
For a good range of eco-friendly
flooring options

CLOTHING
Seasalt
www.seasaltcornwall.co.uk
Lovely range – organic cotton,
bamboo and hemp clothing

Natural Collection
www.naturalcollection.com
Green/eco store including good
range of clothing

Bam Bamboo Clothing
www.bambooclothing.co.uk
Great range of clothes made with
silky bamboo fabric

Planet Earth
www.planetearthstreetwear.com
Green Label clothing range: organic
clothing aimed at the young, urban
male

Greenfibres
www.greenfibres.com
Sumptuous silk and cashmere
undies as well as a good range of
organic everyday wear

Garthenor Organic New Wool
www.organicpurewool.co.uk
Organic wool supplier

Myriad
www.myriadonline.co.uk
Organic yarn supplier

Shetland Sheep and Angora Rabbitry
www.mountainspunfarm.tripod.com
For unusual yarns

Rawganique
www.rawganique.com
Sell organic hemp clothing

PERSONAL CARE
Beauty
Free Spirit Organics
www.freespiritorganics.co.uk
Gorgeous range of organic skincare and beauty products, including a great range of SLS-free haircare products

Hedgerow Herbals
www.hedgerowherbals.com
Bath oils and soaks

Mountain Rose Herbs
www.mountainroseherbs.com
Wonderful range of bath scrubs and ingredients

Organic Bath Co.
www.organicbathco.com
Fabulous bath products

The Organic Herb Trading Company
www.organicherbtrading.com
Supplier of herbs

Greenpeople
www.greenpeople.co.uk
Stock a range of organic lipsticks

Nvey Eco UK
www.nveyeco.co.uk
A fabulous range of organic make-up

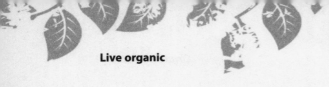

Pit-Rok
www.pitrok.co.uk
Paraben and aluminium free
deodorant

Crystal Spring
www.crystalspringltd.co.uk
Paraben and aluminium free
deodorant

Dr Hauschka
www.drhauschka.co.uk
Skin care

Lavera
www.lavera.co.uk
Cosmetics and skin care. They also
carry a range aimed at men.

LoveLula.com
www.lovelula.com
A wide variety of organic make-up

Logona
www.logona.co.uk
Make-up in a lovely range of

colours, free from parabens,
phthalates, petroleum and mineral
based oils, synthetic fragrances,
colours and preservatives

Suncoat
www.suncoatproducts.com
Organic roll-on eye shadows

Barefoot botanicals Ltd
www.barefoot-botanicals.com
A range of 100% natural skincare
products

The Green People Company Ltd
www.greenpeople.co.uk
Natural and organic
healthy/beauty/cleaning products

Origins Organics
www.origins.co.uk
Skin, body and haircare products

Spirit of Nature
www.spiritofnature.co.uk
Huge range of health and beauty
items

Spiezia Organics

www.spieziaorganics.com

Beauty products, specially aimed at sensitive skins

Free Spirit Organics

www.freespiritorganics.co.uk

Supplier of skin creams

Rose Pure

www.rosepure.com

Make a lovely face lotion with rosehip oil

Miessence

www.miessenceproducts.com

Suppliers of a great facial serum

Raw Gaia

www.rawgaia.com

Rio Trading

www.riohealth.co.uk

Organix

www.organixshop.com

Suppliers of Thera Neem soap, and more

Men's products

Herban Cowboy

www.herbancowboy.com

Florame Aromatherapy

www.florame.co.uk

Health

Neal's Yard Remedies

www.nealsyardremedies.com

Full aromatherapy range; herbs and tinctures

Sex life

Sensua

www.sensua.com

Make organic unflavoured or fruit-flavoured lubricant

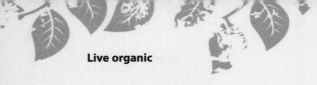

Yes
www.yesyesyes.org
Organic lubricant

Organic Pleasures
www.organicpleasures.co.uk
Sells organic, non-toxic sex toys (all toys free from phthalates and PVC) and products

Sanitary products
Natracare
www.natracare.com
Unbleached organic pads

Luna Pads
www.lunapads.com

Glad Rags
www.gladrags.com

Nappies and baby care
Swaddlebees
www.swaddlebees.com
Organic cotton velour nappies

Pur Babies
www.pur-babies.co.uk
Produce a 100% organic nappy balm and have an organic range

Natural Child
www.naturalchild.co.uk
Produce organic nappy balm

Free Spirit Organics
www.freespritorganics.co.uk
Lovely baby 'faerie' bubbles

Sckoon
www.sckoon.com
Good range of organic toys

Little Green Earthlets
www.earthlets.co.uk
Sell a good range of organic baby goods including cot mattresses

Little Eco-Warriors
www.littleecowarriors.co.uk
Lots of eco baby and child goods

California Baby
www.californiababy.com
For lovely baby bath products

Baby Food
Organix
www.organix.com
A wide range of foods for babies
and young children

Hipp
www.hipp.co.uk
Provide ready-made baby and
toddler food

Plum Organics
www.plumorganics.com
An interesting range of frozen
children's foods

PETS
Pet Planet
www.petplanet.co.uk
Pet supplies including the World's
Best Cat Litter

Bio Catolet
www.fill-my-bowl.co.uk
Cellulose cat litter

Swheat scoop
www.swheatscoop.co.uk
Wheat-based cat litter

MTN Meadowspet
www.mtnmeadowspet.com
Wheatgrass for indoor kitties

Cloud 9
www.tonkatinkers.com
Herbal shampoo for your pet

Earthbath
www.earthbath.com
Produce shampoos and solid bars
of shampoo with organic
ingredients for pets too!

Aubrey Organics
www.aubrey-organics.com
Produce organic treatments for pets

Karma Organic Dry Dog Food
www.wellbeings.com

Timberwolf Organics
www.timberwolforganics.com
Aims to produce dog food as close
to a wild wolf's as possible

www.organicbirdfood.com
Organic bird food and treats

Natura Pet
www.naturapet.com
Offers a good range of pet foods
and treats

Yarrah
www.yarrah.com
Produce a range of organic dry cat
food biscuits and tinned meat
products

Rawganique (see clothing) also sell
a range of hemp products for pets

MISCELLANEOUS
The Hemp Shop
www.thehempshop.co.uk
Supplies fabric, paper, clothing,
foodstuff and toiletries

The Soap School
www.meltandpoursupplies.com
Ways to make your own bath
products, instructions and
workshops

Brighton biofuels
www.brightonbiofuels.com
A good place to find out more
about 'green' fuel

Sheds
www.shedblog.co.uk
An amazing variety of sheds from
the conventional to the totally
amazing

Read more

Cynthia Alquhist (ed.), *Llewellyn's Organic Gardening Almanac: Gardening by the Moon*, Llewellyn Publications, 1996

D.C. Beard, *Shelters, Shacks, and Shanties*. Originally published in 1914, Dover edition, 2004

Rachel Carson, *Silent Spring*, Penguin Modern Classics, 2000

Wendy Cook, *The Biodynamic Food and Cookbook: Real Nutrition That Doesn't Cost the Earth*, Clairview Books, 2006

Jeff Cox and Howard Stevens, *The Organic Cooks Bible: How to Select and Cook the Best Ingredients on the Market*, Wiley, 2006

Kenyon Gibson, *Hemp for Victory*, Whitaker Publishing, 2004

Dan Jason, *The Whole Organic Food Book: Safe, Healthy Harvest from Your Garden to Your Plate*, Raincoast Books, 2002

Leslie Kenton, *The Raw Energy Bible: Packed with Raw Energy Goodness and Food Combining Facts*, Vermilion, 1998

Daphne Lambert, *Little Red Gooseberries: Organic Recipes from Penrhos*, Orion, 2001

Clare Maxwell-Hudson, *The Natural Beauty Book*, Macdonald and Janes, 1976

Mary Muryn, *Water Magic*, Prentice Hall, 1995

Judy Ridgway, *Sprouting Beans and Seeds: with over 150 recipes*, Century Publishing, 1984

231

Ellen Highsmith Silver, *Floorquilts: Fabric Decoupaged Floorcloths – No Sew Fun*, C & T Publishing, 2007

Rudolph Steiner, *What is Biodynamics? A Way to Heal and Revitalize the Earth*, Rudolph Steiner Press, 2007 edition

Sue Stickland, *Heritage Vegetables – The Gardener's Guide to Cultivating Diversity*, Gaia Books Ltd, 1998

Maria Thun, *The Biodynamic Year: Increasing Yield, Quality and Flavour – 100 Helpful Tips for the Gardener or Smallholder*, Temple Lodge Publishing, 2007

Joan Weiskopf, *Pet Food Nation: The Smart, Easy, and Healthy Way to Feed Your Pet Now*, Collins, 2007

Hilary Wright, *Biodynamic Gardening: For Health and Taste*, Mitchell Beazley, 2003

The end...

Or is it a new beginning?

We hope that these ideas will have helped you get excited about making organic changes in your life. Whether you're new to organic living or a seasoned downshifter we hope you've found something here to inspire you. We hope you'll notice changes in your consumer and lifestyle habits and maybe even improvements to your health.

So why not let us know about it? Tell us how you got on. What did it for you – which ideas really made you feel like you could make a difference? Maybe you've got some tips of your own that you'd like to share. And if you liked this book you may find we have even more brilliant ideas that could help change other areas of your life for the better.

You'll find the Infinite Ideas crew waiting for you online at www.infideas.com

Or if you prefer to write, then send your letters to:
Live organic
Infinite Ideas Ltd
36 St Giles, Oxford, OX1 3LD, United Kingdom

We want to know what you think, because we're all working on making our lives better too. Give us your feedback and you could win a copy of another **52 Brilliant Ideas** book of your choice. Or maybe get a crack at writing your own.

Good luck. Be brilliant.

Offer one

Cash in your ideas

We hope you enjoy this book. We hope it inspires, amuses, educates and entertains you. But we don't assume that you're a novice, or that this is the first book that you've bought on the subject. You've got ideas of your own. Maybe our author has missed an idea that you use successfully. If so, why not send it to yourauthormissedatrick@infideas.com, and if we like it we'll post it on our bulletin board. Better still, if your idea makes it into print we'll send you four books of your choice or the cash equivalent. You'll be fully credited so that everyone knows you've had another Brilliant Idea.

Offer two

How could you refuse?

Amazing discounts on bulk quantities of Infinite Ideas books are available to corporations, professional associations and other organisations.

For details call us on:
+44 (0)1865 514888
Fax: +44 (0)1865 514777
or email: info@infideas.com

Where it's at...